KETO DIET BOOK - UK

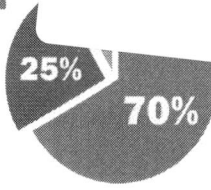

25%
70%

Simple and Healthy Keto Diet Recipes Easy to Follow and Good for Your Health

ISBN: 9798561319280

Table of contents

Dinner recipes

Keto Bonus Recipe

Introduction

For hundreds of thousands of years, people ate mostly meat and vegetables—the so-called caveman diet. With the onset of modern civilization and the development of agriculture, the human body was asking to digest and metabolize more massive amounts of starches and refined sugars. But our bodies are unable to utilize a large number of carbohydrates. Therefore, symptoms develop. The good news is that the ketogenic diet offers a solution—a practical and healthy method for reversing the modern plague of poor health and obesity.

What Is a Keto Diet?

The keto diet has become the most popular low-carb plan, but it may not be the best diet for everyone. That's because it's the strictest, and some may find it challenging to adhere to the optimal daily amounts of carbs, protein, and fat. The goal of the keto diet is to maintain a state of ketosis. For many people, Ketosis can be achieved by reducing carbohydrates to less than 50 grams per day. However, some people find they need to decrease carb limits to as low as 20 to 30 grams a day and maintain a deeper state of ketosis to lose weight.

How the Keto Diet Works?

The primary source of energy for the body is glucose, and this glucose is deriving from the breakdown of carbohydrates that we consume in our diet. As long as it's available, the body will use it first, since it's the quickest to metabolize. However, when your body doesn't have enough carbs for the energy that's needed, it will start to burn fat. The ketogenic diet aims to cause the body to burn fat as its primary source. Is why we limit carbohydrate intake as much as possible to prevent the body from using it as energy's primary source but to burn stored fat instead?

Biologically, the human body has three storehouses of energy for use in times of caloric deficiency: carbohydrate, protein, and fat. Carbohydrate is store as glycogen in the muscle and liver; protein also can be converted to glucose in the liver and used for energy, and fat is stored mainly as body fat. However, there is an alternative fuel for the body, called ketones, which is using only when blood sugar (glucose) is in short supply.

ALL forms of carbohydrates, be it grains, sugar, starchy foods, fruits, and vegetables, are broken down into glucose and stored as glycogen in the body. Excess glycogen that isn't presently needed by the body for energy is store in the liver and the muscles. If the liver and muscles are full, the excess glycogen is then converted into triglycerides (fat molecules) and stored in your blood. But this is not good at all, as it can lead to heart disease. That is why when people on the keto diet restrict carb consumption, they reduce blood triglycerides significantly and consequently lower their risk of heart disease.

Now back to the main subject: Glucose can only be store in our muscles and liver for 24 hours. After a while, the liver starts to produce ketones as the primary fuel source for the body. Ketones or ketone bodies are generated from the breakdown of fatty acids in the liver when glucose becomes unavailable. Ketones, are in fact, produced in minute amounts whenever we go without food for several hours; for instance, after a full night's sleep. Nevertheless, the liver produces more ketones during fasting or when carbohydrate intake drops below 40 grams per day.

A keto diet is designed specifically to result in ketosis where your entire metal- holism will switch over to using ketones as fuel instead of glucose. Remember, the golden formula of this diet is low carb, high fat, and moderate protein.

Keto diet benefits

Being on a low-carb, high-fat diet comes with numerous benefits, as mentioned earlier. Let's consider a few:

Weight Loss

The ketogenic diet uses body fat as an energy source. That is a significant drop in the insulin (the hormone responsible for storing fat) levels. Consequently, your body begins to burn its own stored fat for energy, leading to weight loss. Unlike starvation, which often leads to massive loss of body protein, mainly from muscle tissue, the keto diet provides quick and easy weight loss while allowing dieters to eat as much fat as they desire with minimal protein.

It is a significant benefit of the weight loss ketogenic diet on account of the lower insulin levels and the body's act of burning stored fat. The aim of this diet for weight loss is 'eat fat to lose fat.' Consequently, you will record weight loss every single week of being on a diet, particularly in the first month. You will not be bothered about regaining your lost weight as long as you stick to the keto diet formula of eating high fat, low carb, and moderate proteins. Additionally, some blood pressure issues are linked with excess weight, which is a good thing since keto leads to weight loss

Control Blood Sugar

Since the keto diet is selective on the kind of foods to eat, it naturally results in lower blood sugar levels. Studies have shown that this diet compared to short- calorie diets are better at managing and preventing diabetes. Individuals who are type 2 diabetes but who aren't on insulin can benefit from the ketogenic diet.

Mental Focus

If you are thinking of increasing your mental performance, consider the ketogenic diet. Ketones, the product of this diet, are perfect for the brain. Also, lowering carb intake makes it possible to avoid an increase in blood sugar, which helps you to focus and concentrate significantly.

Normalized Hunger & Increased Energy

Other diets make people feel miserable due to hunger, and they eventually give up. But with the low carb, high-fat diet, you experience an automatic reduction in appetite; you will eat fewer calories effortlessly and surprisingly feel satisfied.   Additionally, you can say good-bye to ups and downs. With the keto diet, you will notice stability in your energy levels. You will always have a full tank of energy to run your day. Your physical performance will be enhanced.

Cholesterol Benefits

Although the ketogenic diet is high in fat, it won't raise your cholesterol or increase your risk for heart disease because the fats are heart-healthy fats or 'good fats' and not trans fats that may lead to inflammation, which causes heart disease. The keto diet leads to a significant increase in blood levels of HDL.

Improved Skin Condition

It's familiar to experience improvements in your skin when you switch to a ketogenic diet. Studies have shown an improvement in acne, skin inflammations, and lesions.
For most people, the keto diet is safe. However, people on diabetes medication, especially those on insulin, need to consult their doctor because their insulin dosages will need to be adjusted. Also, the keto diet is not considered safe pregnant and nursing mothers, as well as those with high blood pressure.

What to eat a Ketogenic Diet?

Different types of food fall into this list. These food ideas push for high-fat content, while at the same time packing other nutrients and healthy vitamins in for the body's use

Vegetables – Fresh vegetables are rich in nutrients and low in calories, which makes them an excellent addition to any diet. With the ketogenic diet, however, you need to be careful about carbs, so stick to leafy greens and low glycemic veggies rather than root vegetables and other starchy veggies. I placed avocados in this section because some of us may recognize it as a vegetable even though it is a fruit.

- Artichokes
- Asparagus
- Avocado
- Bell peppers
- Broccoli
- Cabbage
- Cauliflower

- Cucumber
- Celery
- Kohlrabi
- Lettuce
- Okra or ladies' fingers
- Radishes

- Seaweed
- Spinach
- Tomatoes
- Watercress
- Zucchini

Fruits: Blackberries, cranberries, raspberries, lemon, lime, coconut, and tomatoes.

Meat & Poultry: Beef, pork, game, lamb, and veal, chicken, turkey, and duck.

Ground meat: Pork, beef, turkey, and mixed ground meat.

Lunch & Deli Meats: Bacon, pancetta, pepperoni, salami, suppressant, chorizo, ham, pastrami, prosciutto, and speck. In moderation: bologna and mortadella.

Seafood: Fatty fish, white fish, lobster, crab, shrimp, scallops, mussels, squid, oysters, and octopus.

Dairy: cheese, bleu, mozzarella, brie, Colby cheese, goat, provolone, Gouda, Muenster, camembert, and Swiss cheese; cream, cream cheese, half-and-half; butter and ghee; eggs. In moderation: milk, cheddar, feta, Pepper Jack cheese, full-fat Greek yogurt, crème Fraiche, mascarpone, pot cheese, soured cream, and ricotta.

Herbs and Spices – Fresh herbs and dried spices are an excellent way to flavor your foods without adding any significant number of calories or carbohydrates

- Basil
- Black pepper
- Cayenne
- Cardamom
- Chili powder
- Cilantro
- Cinnamon
- Cumin
- Curry powder
- Garam masala
- Ginger
- Garlic
- Nutmeg
- Oregano
- Onion
- Paprika
- Parsley
- Rosemary
- Sea salt
- Sage
- Thyme
- Turmeric
- White pepper

Nuts & Seeds: peanuts, almonds, walnuts, Brazil nuts, pecans, hazelnuts, macadamia nuts, pine nuts, chia seeds, hemp seeds, pumpkin seeds, and sunflower seeds.

Fats & Oils: copra oil, avocado oil, olive oil, linseed oil, cocoa butter, and nut oil; lard, duck fat, schmaltz, and tallow.

Keto-friendly drink options: Coffee, tea, diet soda, seltzer, soda water, keto smoothies, zero carb energy drinks

Sauces & Condiments: Mayonnaise, mustard, spaghetti sauce, vinegar, and sauce (make bound to check the nutrition facts label).

Canned food: tuna anchovies, crab, salmon, sardines, tomato, sauerkraut, pickles, and olives (make bound to check the nutrition facts label).

Baking ingredients: almond flour, coconut flour, leaven, bicarbonate of soda, cocoa, vanilla, bittersweet chocolate, glucomannan powder.

Nut & Seed Butters: spread, almond butter, hazelnut butter, macadamia spread, coconut butter, pecan butter, edible seed butter, walnut butter, and tahini.

Vegetarian: Tempeh, tofu, full-fat coconut milk, jackfruit, nutritional yeast, Shirataki noodles, Nori sheets, roasted seaweed, Kelp noodles, Kelp flakes.

Keto-Friendly Alcohol: Whiskey, brandy, dry martini, vodka, and tequila.

Seaweed: Wakame, chlorella, nori, doles, spirulina, and kelp.

Keto Sweeteners: Stevia drops, Erythritol, and Monk fruit are zero carb sweeteners; Splenda (sucralose-based sweetener) has 0.5g of carbs per packet (1 g); Erythritol has 4 grams of carbs per teaspoon (4 grams); Xylitol has 4 grams of carbs per teaspoon (4 grams);

Beverages – You should avoid all sweetened drinks on the ketogenic diet, but there are certain beverages that you can still have to add a little more variety to your choice of liquids besides good old water.

- Almond milk unsweetened
- Bone broth
- Cashew milk unsweetened
- Coconut milk
- Club soda
- Coffee
- Herbal tea
- Mineral water
- Seltzer water
- Tea

Foods to Avoid on a Keto Diet

Here is a quick list of some of the primary foods you'll need to avoid on the ketogenic diet

All-purpose flour
Baking mix
Wheat flour
Pastry flour
Cake flour
Cereal
Pasta
Rice
Corn
Baked goods
Corn syrup
Snack bars
Quinoa

Buckwheat
Barley
Couscous
Oats
Muesli
Margarine
Canola oil
Hydrogenated oils
Bananas
Mangos
Pineapple
Potatoes
Sweet potatoes

Candy
Milk chocolate
Ice cream
Sports drinks
Juice cocktail
Soda
Beer
Milk
Low-fat dairy
White sugar
Brown sugar
Maple syrup
Honey

How to Get Started

You've decided to try low-carb or keto. Now what? The first thing is to make sure you have the right mind-set. It's got to be something you want to do, and you need to have a clear image of what you want to achieve. Whether it's losing weight or improving health, you must set an attainable and measurable goal to focus. You also need to commit to the plan and be willing to change your lifestyle for good.

For those new to low-carb, it's best to start by using a food journal so you can track everything you're eating. When I returned to low-carb in 2010, I used a popular weight loss app to keep track of everything I ate. The program made sure I had the calorie deficit needed to meet my weight loss goals, but that app wasn't specific to low-carb, so it didn't track my optimal daily targets for carbs, protein, and fat. However, with keto being so popular these days, there are a ton of keto diet apps that have a lot more features and are specially designed for getting the right daily macro percentages.

After a week or two of keeping a food journal, you'll begin to learn when you should eat, how much of each food to eat, and what you shouldn't eat. You'll also learn how to consume the ideal macronutrient (fat, protein, carbs) ratio for each meal. If journaling becomes too tedious, you can try a few days without it and see how it goes. For the best results, though, I recommend continuing to keep track of what you're eating until you reach your goal. It's easy to go off track if you aren't using some food journal to hold yourself accountable for the things you're eating.

28-Days Keto Diet Weight Loss Challenge

First Week Meal Plan

DAYS	BREAKFAST	LUNCH	DINNER
Sunday	Detoxifying green smoothie (Page No: 23)	Chicken zoodle alfredo (Page No: 38)	Turkey Meatball (Page No: 72)
Monday	Lemon flaxseed muffins (Page No: 16)	Chicken zoodle alfredo (Page No: 38)	Turkey Meatball (Page No: 72)
Tuesday	Lemon flaxseed muffins (Page No: 16)	Spiced pumpkin soup (Page No: 61)	Tasty Salted Turnip Fries (Page No: 81)
Wednesday	Detoxifying green smoothie (Page No: 23)	Spiced pumpkin soup (Page No: 61)	Tasty Salted Turnip Fries (Page No: 81)
Thursday	Crispy chai waffles (Page No: 25)	Baked chicken nuggets (Page No: 39)	Overnight Oats (Page No: 82)
Friday	Kale avocado smoothie (Page No: 19)	Baked chicken nuggets (Page No: 39)	Peanut Butter Biscuits (Page No: 68)
Saturday	Almond butter muffins (Page No: 20)	Chicken zoodle alfredo (Page No: 38)	Peanut Butter Biscuits (Page No: 68)

28-Days Keto Diet Weight Loss Challenge

Second Week Meal Plan

DAYS	BREAKFAST	LUNCH	DINNER
Sunday	Detoxifying green smoothie (Page No: 23)	Spiced pumpkin soup (Page No: 61)	Turkey Meatball (Page No: 72)
Monday	Lemon flaxseed muffins (Page No: 16)	Chicken zoodle alfredo (Page No: 38)	Overnight Oats (Page No: 82)
Tuesday	Detoxifying green smoothie (Page No: 23)	Spiced pumpkin soup (Page No: 61)	Tasty Salted Turnip Fries (Page No: 81)
Wednesday	Lemon flaxseed muffins (Page No: 16)	Baked chicken nuggets (Page No: 39)	Tasty Salted Turnip Fries (Page No: 81)
Thursday	Kale avocado smoothie (Page No: 19)	Chicken zoodle alfredo (Page No: 38)	Peanut Butter Biscuits (Page No: 68)
Friday	Crispy chai waffles (Page No: 25)	Baked chicken nuggets (Page No: 39)	Turkey Meatball (Page No: 72)
Saturday	Almond butter muffins (Page No: 20)	Fried salmon cakes (Page No: 42)	Overnight Oats (Page No: 82)

28-Days Keto Diet Weight Loss Challenge

Third Week Meal Plan

DAYS	BREAKFAST	LUNCH	DINNER
Sunday	Crispy chai waffles (Page No: 25)	Fried salmon cakes (Page No: 42)	Tasty Salted Turnip Fries (Page No: 81)
Monday	Crispy chai waffles (Page No: 25)	Chicken zoodle alfredo (Page No: 38)	Tasty Salted Turnip Fries (Page No: 81)
Tuesday	Kale avocado smoothie (Page No: 19)	Spiced pumpkin soup (Page No: 61)	Overnight Oats (Page No: 82)
Wednesday	Detoxifying green smoothie (Page No: 23)	Spiced pumpkin soup (Page No: 61)	Peanut Butter Biscuits (Page No: 68)
Thursday	Detoxifying green smoothie (Page No: 23)	Baked chicken nuggets (Page No: 39)	Turkey Meatball (Page No: 72)
Friday	Lemon flaxseed muffins (Page No: 16)	Fried salmon cakes (Page No: 42)	Overnight Oats (Page No: 82)
Saturday	Lemon flaxseed muffins (Page No: 16)	Chicken zoodle alfredo (Page No: 38)	Turkey Meatball (Page No: 72)

28-Days Keto Diet Weight Loss Challenge

Fourth Week Meal Plan

DAYS	BREAKFAST	LUNCH	DINNER
Sunday	Detoxifying green smoothie (Page No: 23)	Spiced pumpkin soup (Page No: 61)	Turkey Meatball (Page No: 72)
Monday	Detoxifying green smoothie (Page No: 23)	Spiced pumpkin soup (Page No: 61)	Overnight Oats (Page No: 82)
Tuesday	Lemon flaxseed muffins (Page No: 16)	Baked chicken nuggets (Page No: 39)	Peanut Butter Biscuits (Page No: 68)
Wednesday	Lemon flaxseed muffins (Page No: 16)	Fried salmon cakes (Page No: 42)	Turkey Meatball (Page No: 72)
Thursday	Kale avocado smoothie (Page No: 19)	Chicken zoodle alfredo (Page No: 38)	Overnight Oats (Page No: 82)
Friday	Crispy chai waffles (Page No: 25)	Baked chicken nuggets (Page No: 39)	Tasty Salted Turnip Fries (Page No: 81)
Saturday	Almond butter muffins (Page No: 20)	Chicken zoodle alfredo (Page No: 38)	Tasty Salted Turnip Fries (Page No: 81)

Breakfast recipes

Strawberry rhubarb pie smoothie

Prep time: 5 minutes
Cook time: none
Servings:

Ingredients:

- One small stalk rhubarb, sliced
- ¼ cup frozen sliced strawberries
- ¾ cup unsweetened cashew milk
- ½ cup full-fat yogurt, plain
- 1 ounce of raw almonds
- ½ teaspoon vanilla extract
- Liquid stevia extract, to taste

Instructions:

1. Combine the rhubarb, strawberries, and almond milk in a blender.
2. Pulse the ingredients several times.
3. Add the remaining ingredients and blend until smooth.
4. Pour into a large glass and enjoy immediately.

Nutrition info:
285 calories, 20g fat, 11g protein, 17.5g carbs, 5g fiber, 12.5g net carbs

Breakfast recipes

Lemon flaxseed muffins

Prep time: 10 minutes
Cook time: 20 minutes
Servings: 12

Ingredients:

- ¾ cups almond flour
- ¼ cup ground flaxseed
- ¼ cup powdered erythritol
- One teaspoon baking powder
- ⅛ teaspoon salt
- ¼ cup canned coconut milk
- ¼ cup coconut oil, melted

- ¼ cup fresh lemon juice
- Three large eggs
- Two tablespoons grated lemon peel

Instructions:

1. Preheat the oven to 350°f and line a muffin pan with paper liners.
2. Whisk the almond flour together with the ground flaxseed, erythritol, baking powder, and salt in a mixing bowl.
3. In a separate bowl, whisk together the coconut milk, coconut oil, lemon juice, and eggs.
4. Stir the wet ingredients into the dry until just combined.
5. Fold in the grated lemon peel.
6. Spoon the batter into the prepared pan and bake for 18 to 20 minutes until a knife inserted in the center comes out clean.
7. Cool the muffins in the pan for 5 minutes, then turn out onto a wire cooling rack.

Nutrition info:
120 calories, 11g fat, 3.5g protein, 3g carbs, 1.5g fiber, 1.5g net carbs

Breakfast recipes

Sesame Pork Lettuce Wraps

Prep Time: 10 minutes
Cook Time: 15 minutes
Servings: 4

Ingredients

- One tablespoon olive oil
- ¼ cup diced yellow onion
- ¼ cup chopped green pepper
- Two tablespoons diced celery
- 6 ounces ground pork
- ¼ teaspoon onion powder
- ¼ teaspoon garlic powder
- Two tablespoons soy sauce
- One teaspoon sesame oil
- Four leaves butter lettuce, separated
- One tablespoon toasted sesame seed

Instructions

1. Heat the oil in a skillet over medium heat.

2. Add the onions, peppers, and celery and sauté for 5 minutes until tender.
3. Stir in the pork and cook until just browned.
4. Add the onion powder and garlic powder, then stir in the soy sauce and sesame oil.
5. Season with salt and pepper to taste, then remove from heat.
6. Place the lettuce leaves on a plate and spoon the pork mixture evenly into them.
7. Sprinkle with sesame seeds to serve.

Nutrition info:
Calories: 500 Fat: 29 g Protein: 49 g Total Carbs: 10.5 g Fiber: 3 g Net Carbs: 7.5 g

Breakfast recipes

Easy Cheeseburger salad

Prep Time: 10 minutes
Cook Time: 10 minutes
Servings: 2

Ingredients

- 7 ounces ground beef
- Salt and pepper
- Three tablespoons mayonnaise
- One tablespoon diced pickles
- One teaspoon mustard
- ½ teaspoon ketchup
- Pinch smoked paprika
- 3 ounces chopped romaine lettuce
- 1/3 cup diced tomatoes
- ¼ cup shredded cheddar cheese

Instructions

1. Brown the ground beef over high heat then season with salt and pepper to taste.
2. Drain the fat from the beef and remove from heat.
3. Combine the mayonnaise, pickles, mustard, ketchup, and paprika in a blender.
4. Blend the mixture until smooth and well combined.
5. Combine the lettuce, tomatoes, and cheddar cheese in a mixing bowl.
6. Toss in the ground beef and the dressing until evenly coated.

Nutrition info:
Calories: 395 Fat: 27.5 g Protein: 27.5 g Total Carbs: 9 g Fiber: 1 g Net Carbs: 8 g

Breakfast recipes

Kale avocado smoothie

Prep time: 5 minutes
Cook time: 15
Servings: 2

Ingredients:

- 1 cup fresh chopped kale
- ½ cup chopped avocado
- ¾ cup unsweetened almond milk
- ¼ cup full-fat yogurt, plain
- 3 to 4 ice cubes
- One tablespoon fresh lemon juice
- Liquid stevia extract, to taste

Instructions:

1. Combine the kale, avocado, and almond milk in a blender.
2. Pulse the ingredients several times.
3. Add the remaining ingredients and blend until smooth.
4. Pour into a large glass and enjoy immediately.

Nutrition info:
250 calories, 19g fat, 6g protein, 17.5g carbs, 6.5g fiber, 11g net carbs

Breakfast recipes

Bacon breakfast bombs

Prep Time: 40 minutes
Cook Time: 0 minutes
Servings: 4

Ingredients

- Six slices thick-cut bacon
- Four large eggs
- ¼ cup cubed butter
- Two tablespoons mayonnaise
- Salt and pepper

Instructions

1. Cook the bacon in a large skillet over medium-high heat until crisp.

2. Let the bacon cool a little, then chop it up and set it aside, reserving the bacon grease.
3. Fill a saucepan with water and a pinch of salt, then bring to a boil.
4. Add the eggs and boil them for 10 minutes before transferring to an ice water bath.
5. Let the eggs cool, then peel them and chop them coarsely.
6. Mash the chopped eggs with the butter, then stir in the mayonnaise, salt, and pepper.
7. Stir in the reserved bacon grease, then cover the mixture and chill for 30 minutes.
8. Divide the egg mixture into six portions and roll them into balls, then roll in the crushed bacon.
9. Serve immediately and store the leftovers in the fridge.

Nutrition info:
Calories: 535 Fat: 49 g Protein: 21 g Total Carbs: 4.5 g Fiber: 0 g Net Carbs: 4.5 g

Breakfast recipes

Beets and blueberry smoothie

Prep time: 5 minutes
Cook time: none
Servings: 1

Ingredients:

- 1 cup unsweetened coconut milk
- ¼ cup heavy cream
- ¼ cup frozen blueberries
- One small beet, peeled and chopped
- One teaspoon chia seeds
- Liquid stevia extract, to taste

Instructions:

1. Combine the blueberries, beets, and coconut milk in a blender.
2. Pulse the ingredients several times.
3. Add the remaining ingredients and blend until smooth.
4. Pour into a large glass and enjoy immediately.

Nutrition info:
215 calories, 17g fat, 2.5g protein, 15g carbs, 5g fiber, 10g net carbs

Breakfast recipes

Almond butter muffins

Prep time: 10 minutes

Cook time: 25 minutes
Servings: 12

Ingredients:

- 2 cups almond flour
- 1 cup powdered erythritol
- Two teaspoons baking powder
- ¼ teaspoon salt
- ¾ cup almond butter, warmed
- ¾ cup unsweetened almond milk
- Four large eggs

Instructions:

1. Preheat the oven to 350°f and line a muffin pan with paper liners.
2. Whisk the almond flour together with the erythritol, baking powder, and salt in a mixing bowl.
3. In a separate bowl, whisk together the almond milk, almond butter, and eggs.
4. Stir the wet ingredients into the dry until just combined.
5. Spoon the batter into the prepared pan and bake for 22 to 25 minutes until a knife inserted in the center comes out clean.
6. Cool the muffins in the pan for 5 minutes, then turn out onto a wire cooling rack.

Nutrition info:

135 calories, 11g fat, 6g protein, 4g carbs, 2g fiber, 2g net Carbs

Breakfast recipes

Classic western omelet

Prep time: 5 minutes
Cook time: 10 minutes
Servings: 1

Ingredients:

- Two teaspoons coconut oil
- Three large eggs whisked
- One tablespoon heavy cream
- Salt and pepper
- ¼ cup diced green pepper
- ¼ cup diced yellow onion
- ¼ cup diced ham

Instructions:

1. Whisk together the eggs, heavy cream, salt, and pepper in a small bowl.
2. Heat 1 teaspoon coconut oil in a small skillet over medium heat.
3. Add the peppers, onions, and ham, then sauté for 3 to 4 minutes.
4. Spoon the mixture into a bowl and reheat the skillet with the rest of the oil.
5. Pour in the whisked eggs and cook until the bottom of the egg starts to set.
6. Tilt the pan to spread the egg and cook until almost set.
7. Spoon the veggie and ham mixture over half the omelet and fold it over.
8. Let the omelet cook until the eggs set, then serve hot.

Nutrition info:
415 calories, 32.5g fat, 25g protein, 6.5g carbs, 1.5g fiber, 5g net carbs

Breakfast recipes

Mushroom Soup with Fried egg

Prep Time: 5 minutes
Cook Time: 15 minutes
Servings: 4

Ingredients

- One teaspoon olive oil
- Four white mushrooms, sliced thin
- 100 grams cauliflower, riced
- 1 cup vegetable broth
- Three tablespoons heavy cream
- Two tablespoons shredded cheese
- One teaspoon butter
- Four large egg

Instructions

1. Heat the oil in a small saucepan over medium heat.
2. Add the mushrooms and cook until they are tender about 6 minutes.
3. Stir in the riced cauliflower, vegetable broth, and heavy cream.
4. Season with salt and pepper, then stir in the cheese.
5. Simmer the soup until it thickens to the desired level, then remove from heat.
6. Fry the egg in the butter until cooked to the desired level, then serve over the soup.

Nutrition info:
Calories: 385 Fat: 31 g Protein: 20 g Total Carbs: 10 g Fiber: 3 g Net Carbs: 7 g

Breakfast recipes

Sheet pan eggs with ham and pepper jack

Prep time: 5 minutes
Cook time: 15 minutes
Servings: 6

Ingredients:

- 12 large eggs, whisked
- Salt and pepper
- 2 cups diced ham
- 1 cup shredded pepper jack cheese

Instructions:

1. Preheat the oven to 350°f and grease a rimmed baking sheet with cooking spray.
2. Whisk the eggs in a bowl with salt and pepper until frothy.
3. Stir in the ham and cheese until well combined.
4. Pour the mixture in the baking sheet and spread into an even layer.
5. Bake for 12 to 15 minutes until the egg set.
6. Let cool slightly, then cut into squares to serve.

Nutrition info:
235 calories, 15g fat, 21g protein, 2.5g carbs, 0.5g fiber, 2g net carbs

Breakfast recipes

Detoxifying green smoothie

Prep time: 5 minutes
Cook time: none
Servings: 1

Ingredients:

- 1 cup fresh chopped kale
- ½ cup fresh baby spinach
- ¼ cup sliced celery
- 1 cup of water
- 3 to 4 ice cubes
- Two tablespoons fresh lemon juice
- One tablespoon fresh lime juice
- One tablespoon coconut oil
- Liquid stevia extract, to taste

Instructions:

1. Combine the kale, spinach, and celery in a blender.
2. Pulse the ingredients several times.
3. Add the remaining ingredients and blend until smooth.
4. Pour into a large glass and enjoy immediately.

Nutrition info:

160 calories, 14g fat, 2.5g protein, 8g carbs, 2g fiber, 6g net carbs

Breakfast recipes

Avocado Egg & salami sandwiches

Prep Time: 10 minutes
Cook Time: 10 minutes
Servings: 4

Ingredients

- 4 Easy Cloud Buns
- One teaspoon butter
- Four large eggs
- One medium tomato, sliced into four slices
- 1-ounce fresh mozzarella, sliced thin
- One small avocado, sliced thin
- 2 ounces sliced salami
- Salt and pepper

Instructions

1. Toast the cloud buns on a baking sheet in the oven until golden brown.
2. Heat the butter in a large skillet over medium heat.
3. Crack the eggs into the skillet and season with salt and pepper.
4. Cook the eggs until done to the desired level, then place one on each cloud bun.
5. Top the buns with sliced tomato, mozzarella, avocado, and salami.

Nutrition info:

Calories: 490 Fat: 40.5 g Protein: 22.5 g Total Carbs: 12.5 g Fiber: 7.5 g Net Carbs: 5 g

Breakfast recipes

Crispy chai waffles

Prep time: 10 minutes

Cook time: 20 minutes
Servings: 4

Ingredients:

- Four large eggs, separated into whites and yolks
- Three tablespoons coconut flour
- Three tablespoons powdered erythritol
- One ¼ teaspoon baking powder
- One teaspoon vanilla extract
- ½ teaspoon ground cinnamon
- ¼ teaspoon ground ginger
- Pinch ground cloves
- Pinch ground cardamom
- Three tablespoons coconut oil, melted
- Three tablespoons unsweetened almond milk

Instructions:

1. Separate the eggs into two different mixing bowls.
2. Whip the egg whites until stiff peaks form then set aside.
3. Whisk the egg yolks with the coconut flour, erythritol, baking powder, vanilla, cinnamon, cardamom, and cloves in the other bowl.
4. Add the melted coconut oil to the second bowl while whisking, then whisk in the almond milk.
5. Gently fold in the egg whites until just combined.
6. Preheat the waffle iron and grease with cooking spray.
7. Spoon about ½ cup of batter into the iron.
8. Cook the waffle according to the manufacturer's instructions.
9. Remove the waffle to a plate and repeat with the remaining batter.

Nutrition info:
215 calories, 17g fat, 8g protein, 8g carbs, 4g fiber, 4g net carbs

Breakfast recipes

Broccoli kale egg scramble

Prep time: 5 minutes
Cook time: 10 minutes
Servings: 1

Ingredients:

- Two large eggs whisked
- One tablespoon heavy cream
- Salt and pepper
- One teaspoon coconut oil
- 1 cup fresh chopped kale
- ¼ cup frozen broccoli florets, thawed
- Two tablespoons grated parmesan cheese

Instructions:

1. Whisk the eggs together with the heavy cream, salt, and pepper in a bowl.
2. Heat 1 teaspoon coconut oil in a medium skillet over medium heat.
3. Stir in the kale and broccoli then cook until the kale wilted, about 1 to 2 minutes.
4. Pour in the eggs and cook, occasionally stirring, until just set.
5. Stir in the parmesan cheese and serve hot.

Nutrition info:
315 calories, 23g fat, 19.5g protein, 10g carbs, 1.5g fiber, 8.5g net carbs

Breakfast recipes

Gyro Salad with avo-Tzatziki

Prep Time: 10 minutes
Cook Time: 25 minutes
Servings: 4

Ingredients

- One tablespoon olive oil
- 1 pound ground lamb meat
- ½ medium yellow onion, diced
- ¼ cup chicken broth
- Four teaspoons lemon juice, divided

- ½ teaspoon dried oregano
- ½ teaspoon dried thyme
- ½ English cucumber
- One medium ripe avocado
- Two teaspoons fresh chopped mint
- One teaspoon fresh chopped dill
- 6 cups chopped romaine lettuce

Instructions

1. Heat the oil in a large skillet over medium-high heat and add the lamb.
2. Cook for 3 minutes, stirring often, then stir in the onion.
3. Keep cooking until the lamb is cooked through and the onion softened, then stir in the chicken broth, two teaspoons lemon juice, oregano, and thyme.
4. Season with salt and pepper to taste then simmer for 5 minutes.
5. Grate the cucumber, then spread evenly on a clean towel and wring out the moisture.
6. Place the grated cucumber in a food processor and add the avocado, two teaspoons lemon juice, mint, and dill with a pinch of salt. Blend the mixture until smooth.
7. Serve the gyro meat over chopped lettuce with a spoonful of avo-tzatziki.

Nutrition info:
Calories: 495 Fat: 29 g Protein: 45 g Total Carbs: 13.5 g Fiber: 6 g Net Carbs: 7.5 g

Breakfast recipes

Three cheese egg muffins

Prep time: 5 minutes
Cook time: 25 minutes
Servings: 12

Ingredients:

- One tablespoon butter
- ½ cup diced yellow onion
- 12 large eggs, whisked
- ½ cup of canned coconut milk
- ¼ cup sliced green onion
- Salt and pepper
- ½ cup shredded cheddar cheese
- ½ cup shredded swiss cheese
- ¼ cup grated parmesan cheese

Instructions:

1. Preheat the oven to 350°f and grease a muffin pan with cooking spray.

2. Melt the butter in a medium skillet over medium heat.
3. Add the onions then cook for 3 to 4 minutes until softened.
4. Divide the mixture among the muffin cups.
5. Whisk together the eggs, coconut milk, green onions, salt, and pepper, then spoon into the muffin cups.
6. Combine the three kinds of cheese in a bowl and sprinkle over the egg muffins.
7. Bake for 20 to 25 minutes until the egg set.

Nutrition info:
150 calories, 11.5g fat, 10g protein, 2g carbs, 0.5g fiber, 1.5g net carbs

Breakfast recipes

Pepper Jack Sausage Egg Muffins

Prep Time: 10 minutes
Cook Time: 30 minutes
Servings: 3

Ingredients

- 10 ounces ground breakfast sausage
- ½ cup diced yellow onion
- ¼ teaspoon garlic powder
- Salt and pepper
- Three large eggs whisked
- Two tablespoons heavy cream
- ½ cup shredded pepper jack cheese

Instructions

1. Preheat the oven to 350°F and grease three ramekins with cooking spray.
2. Stir together the ground sausage, diced onion, garlic powder, salt, and pepper in a mixing bowl.
3. Divide the sausage mixture evenly in the ramekins, pressing it into the bottom and sides, leaving the middle open.
4. Whisk together the eggs and heavy cream with salt and pepper.
5. Divide the egg mixture among the sausage cups and top with shredded cheese.
6. Bake for 25 to 30 minutes until the eggs are set, and the cheese browned.

Nutrition info:
Calories: 455 Fat: 37 g Protein: 26 g Total Carbs: 3.5 g Fiber: 0.5 g Net Carbs: 3 g

Breakfast recipes

Cinnamon almond porridge

Prep time: 5 minutes
Cook time: 5 minutes
Servings: 1

Ingredients:

- One tablespoon butter
- One tablespoon coconut flour
- One large egg whisked
- ⅛ teaspoon ground cinnamon
- Pinch salt
- ¼ cup canned coconut milk
- One tablespoon almond butter

Instructions:

1. Melt the butter in a small saucepan over low heat.
2. Whisk in the coconut flour, egg, cinnamon, and salt.
3. Add the coconut milk while whisking and stir in the almond butter until smooth.
4. Simmer on low heat, often stirring, until heated.
5. Spoon into a bowl and serve.

Nutrition info:
470 calories, 42g fat, 13g protein, 15g carbs, 8g fiber, 7g net carbs

Breakfast recipes

Bacon, mushroom, and swiss omelet

Prep time: 5 minutes
Cook time: 10 minutes
Servings: 1

Ingredients:

- Three large eggs whisked
- One tablespoon heavy cream
- Salt and pepper
- Two slices uncooked bacon, chopped
- ¼ cup diced mushrooms
- ¼ cup shredded swiss cheese

Instructions:

1. Whisk together the eggs, heavy cream, salt, and pepper in a small bowl.
2. Cook the bacon in a small skillet over medium-high heat.
3. When the bacon is crisp, spoon it into a bowl.
4. Reheat the skillet over medium heat, then add the mushrooms.
5. Cook the mushrooms until browned, then spoon into the bowl with the bacon.
6. Reheat the skillet with the rest of the oil.
7. Pour in the whisked eggs and cook until the bottom of the egg starts to set.
8. Tilt the pan to spread the egg and cook until almost set.
9. Spoon the bacon and mushroom mixture over half the omelet, then sprinkle with cheese and fold it over.
10. Let the omelet cook until the eggs set, then serve hot.

Nutrition info:
475 calories, 36g fat, 34g protein, 4g carbs, 0.5g fiber, 3.5g net carbs

Breakfast recipes

Maple cranberry muffins

Prep time: 10 minutes
Cook time: 20 minutes
Servings: 3

Ingredients:

- ¾ cups almond flour
- ¼ cup ground flaxseed
- ¼ cup powdered erythritol
- One teaspoon baking powder
- ⅛ teaspoon salt
- ⅓ cup of canned coconut milk
- ¼ cup coconut oil, melted
- Three large eggs
- ½ cup fresh cranberries
- One teaspoon maple extract

Instructions:

1. Preheat the oven to 350°f and line a muffin pan with paper liners.
2. Whisk the almond flour together with the ground flaxseed, erythritol, baking powder, and salt in a mixing bowl.
3. In a separate bowl, whisk together the coconut milk, coconut oil, eggs, and maple extract.
4. Stir the wet ingredients into the dry until just combined, then fold in the cranberries.

5. Spoon the batter into the prepared pan and bake for 18 to 20 minutes until a knife inserted in the center comes out clean.
6. Cool the muffins in the pan for 5 minutes, then turn out onto a wire cooling rack.

Nutrition info:
125 calories, 11.5g fat, 3.5g protein, 3g carbs, 1.5g fiber, 1.5g net carbs

Breakfast recipes

Coco-cashew macadamia muffins

Prep time: 10 minutes
Cook time: 25 minutes
Servings: 4

Ingredients:

- One ¾ cups almond flour
- 1 cup powdered erythritol
- ¼ cup unsweetened cocoa powder
- Two teaspoons baking powder
- ¼ teaspoon salt
- ¾ cup cashew butter, melted
- ¾ cup unsweetened almond milk
- Four large eggs
- ¼ cup chopped macadamia nuts

Instructions:

1. Preheat the oven to 350°f and line a muffin pan with paper liners.
2. Whisk the almond flour together with the erythritol, cocoa powder, baking powder, and salt in a mixing bowl.
3. In a separate bowl, whisk together the almond milk, cashew butter, and eggs.
4. Stir the wet ingredients into the dry until just combined, then fold in the nuts.
5. Spoon the batter into the prepared pan and bake for 22 to 25 minutes until a knife inserted in the center comes out clean.
6. Cool the muffins in the pan for 5 minutes, then turn out onto a wire cooling rack.

Nutrition info:
230 calories, 20g fat, 9g protein, 9g carbs, 2.5g fiber, 6.5gNet carbs

Breakfast recipes

Chocolate protein pancakes

Prep time: 5 minutes
Cook time: 15 minutes
Servings: 4

Ingredients:

- 1 cup of canned coconut milk
- ¼ cup of coconut oil
- Eight large eggs
- Two scoops (40g) egg white protein powder
- ¼ cup unsweetened cocoa powder
- One teaspoon vanilla extract
- Liquid stevia extract, to taste

Instructions:

1. Combine the coconut milk, coconut oil, and eggs in a food processor.
2. Pulse the mixture several times, then add the remaining ingredients.
3. Blend until smooth and well combined – adjust sweetness to taste.
4. Heat a nonstick skillet over medium heat.
5. Spoon in the batter, using about ¼ cup per pancake.
6. Cook until bubbles form on the surface of the batter, then carefully flip.
7. Let the pancake cook until the underside browned.
8. Transfer to a plate to keep warm and repeat with the remaining batter.

Nutrition info:
455 calories, 38.5g fat, 23g protein, 8g carbs, 3g fiber, 5g net carbs

Breakfast recipes

Ham, cheddar, and chive omelet

Prep time: 5 minutes
Cook time: 10 minutes
Servings: 1

Ingredients:

- One teaspoon coconut oil

- Three large eggs whisked

- One tablespoon heavy cream
- One tablespoon chopped chives
- Salt and pepper
- ¼ cup shredded cheddar cheese
- ¼ cup diced ham

Instructions:

1. Whisk together the eggs, heavy cream, chives, salt, and pepper in a small bowl.
2. Heat the coconut oil in a small skillet over medium heat.
3. Pour in the whisked eggs and cook until the bottom of the egg starts to set.
4. Tilt the pan to spread the egg and cook until almost set.
5. Sprinkle the ham and cheddar cheese over half the omelet and fold it over.
6. Let the omelet cook until the eggs set, then serve hot.

Nutrition info:

515 calories, 42g fat, 32g protein, 3.5g carbs, 0.5g fiber, 3g net carbs

Breakfast recipes

Spinach parmesan egg scramble

Prep time: 5 minutes
Cook time: 10 minutes
Servings: 1

Ingredients:

- Two large eggs whisked
- One tablespoon heavy cream
- Salt and pepper
- One teaspoon coconut oil
- 2 cups fresh baby spinach
- Two tablespoons grated parmesan cheese

Instructions:

1. Whisk the eggs together with the heavy cream, salt, and pepper in a bowl.
2. Heat the coconut oil in a medium skillet over medium heat.
3. Stir in the spinach and cook until wilted, about 1 to 2 minutes.
4. Pour in the eggs and cook, occasionally stirring, until just set – about 1 to 2 minutes.
5. Stir in the parmesan and serve hot.

Nutrition info:

290 calories, 23g fat, 18.5g protein, 3.5g carbs, 1.5g fiber, 2g net carbs

Breakfast recipes

Cinnamon roll waffles

Prep time: 10 minutes
Cook time: 20 minutes
Servings: 2

Ingredients:

- Four large eggs, separated into whites and yolks
- Three tablespoons coconut flour
- Three tablespoons powdered erythritol
- One ¼ teaspoon baking powder
- One teaspoon vanilla extract
- ½ teaspoon ground cinnamon
- Pinch ground nutmeg
- ½ cup heavy cream

Instructions:

1. Separate the eggs into two different mixing bowls.
2. Whip the egg whites until stiff peaks form then set aside.
3. Whisk the egg yolks with the coconut flour, erythritol, baking powder, vanilla, cinnamon, and nutmeg in the other bowl.
4. Add the heavy cream, whisking until just combined, then gently fold in the egg whites.
5. Preheat the waffle iron and grease with cooking spray.
6. Spoon about ½ cup of batter into the iron.
7. Cook the waffle according to the manufacturer's instructions.
8. Remove the waffle to a plate and repeat with the remaining batter.

Nutrition info:
350 calories, 24g fat, 16g protein, 16g carbs, 8g fiber, 8g net carbs

Breakfast recipes

Bacon swiss waffles

Prep time: 10 minutes
Cook time: 20 minutes
Servings: 4

Ingredients:

- Six slices uncooked bacon

- Four large eggs, separated into whites and yolks
- Three tablespoons coconut flour
- One ¼ teaspoon baking powder
- Salt and pepper
- Three tablespoons unsweetened almond milk
- ½ cup shredded swiss cheese
- ¼ cup sour cream

Instructions:

1. Cook the bacon in a skillet until crisp, then coarsely chop into a bowl.
2. Spoon out three tablespoons of the bacon grease and set it aside.
3. Separate the eggs into two different mixing bowls.
4. Whip the egg whites until stiff peaks form then set aside.
5. Whisk the egg yolks with the coconut flour, erythritol, baking powder, salt, and pepper in the other bowl.
6. Add the almond milk and bacon grease to the second bowl while whisking, then gently fold in the egg whites until just combined.
7. Stir in the shredded swiss cheese and half the chopped bacon.
8. Preheat the waffle iron and grease with cooking spray.
9. Spoon a heaping ½ cup of batter into the iron.
10. Cook the waffle according to the manufacturer's instructions.
11. Remove the waffle to a plate and repeat with the remaining batter.
12. Serve the waffles topped with sour cream and chopped bacon.

Nutrition info:
250 calories, 16.5g fat, 17g protein, 8g carbs, 4g fiber, 4g net carbs

Breakfast recipes

Meaty breakfast omelet

Prep time: 5 minutes
Cook time: 10 minutes
Servings: 1

Ingredients:

- Three large eggs whisked
- One tablespoon heavy cream
- Salt and pepper
- One slice uncooked bacon, chopped
- 1-ounce breakfast sausage, crumbled
- ¼ cup diced ham

Instructions:

1. Whisk together the eggs, heavy cream, salt, and pepper in a small bowl.
2. Cook the bacon in a small skillet over medium-high heat.
3. When the bacon is crisp, spoon it off into a bowl.
4. Cook the sausage in the skillet until browned, then add to the bowl with the bacon.
5. Reheat the skillet with the grease from the bacon and sausage.
6. Pour in the whisked eggs and cook until the bottom of the egg starts to set.
7. Tilt the pan to spread the egg and cook until almost set.
8. Sprinkle the bacon, sausage, and ham over half the omelet and fold it over.
9. Let the omelet cook until the eggs set, then serve hot.

Nutrition info:

470 calories, 35.5g fat, 34g protein, 3g carbs, 0.5g fiber, 2.5g net carbs

Breakfast recipes

Pumpkin spice waffles

Prep time: 10 minutes
Cook time: 20 minutes
Servings: 2

Ingredients:

- Four large eggs, separated into whites and yolks
- Three tablespoons coconut flour
- Three tablespoons powdered erythritol
- One ¼ teaspoon baking powder
- One teaspoon vanilla extract
- ½ teaspoon ground cinnamon
- ¼ teaspoon ground nutmeg
- Pinch ground cloves
- ½ cup pumpkin puree

Instructions:

1. Separate the eggs into two different mixing bowls.
2. Whip the egg whites until stiff peaks form then set aside.
3. Whisk the egg yolks with the coconut flour, erythritol, baking powder, vanilla, cinnamon, nutmeg, and cloves in the other bowl.
4. Add the pumpkin puree, whisking until combined, then gently fold in the egg whites.
5. Preheat the waffle iron and grease with cooking spray.
6. Spoon about ½ cup of batter into the iron.
7. Cook the waffle according to the manufacturer's instructions.
8. Remove the waffle to a plate and repeat with the remaining batter.

Nutrition info:

265 calories, 13.5g fat, 16g protein, 20g carbs, 10g fiber, 10g net carbs

Lunch recipes

Pan-Fried pepperoni pizzas

Prep Time: 10 minutes
Cook Time: 25 minutes
Servings: 6

Ingredients

- Six large eggs
- Six tablespoons grated parmesan cheese
- Three tablespoons psyllium husk powder
- 1 ½ teaspoon Italian seasoning
- Three tablespoons olive oil
- Nine tablespoons low-carb tomato sauce, divided
- 4 ½ ounces shredded mozzarella, divided
- 1 ½ ounces diced pepperoni, divided
- Three tablespoons fresh chopped basil

Instructions

1. Combine the eggs, parmesan, and psyllium husk powder with the Italian seasoning and a pinch of salt in a blender.
2. Blend until smooth and well combined, about 30 seconds, then rest for 5 minutes.
3. Heat 1 tablespoon of oil in a skillet over medium-high heat.
4. Spoon 1/3 of the batter into the skillet and spread in a circle then cook until browned underneath.
5. Flip the pizza crust and cook until browned on the other side.
6. Remove the crust to a foil-lined baking sheet and repeat with the remaining batter.
7. Spoon 3 tablespoons of low-carb tomato sauce over each crust.
8. Top with diced pepperoni and shredded cheese, then broil until the cheese is browned.
9. Sprinkle with fresh basil, then slice the pizza to serve.

Nutrition info:

Calories: 545 Fat: 42 g Protein: 32 g Total Carbs: 12 g Fiber: 7.5 g Net Carbs: 4.5 g

Lunch recipes

Chicken zoodle alfredo

Prep Time: 10 minutes
Cook Time: 25 minutes
Servings: 3

Ingredients

- 2 (6-ounce) chicken breasts
- One tablespoon olive oil
- Salt and pepper
- Two tablespoons butter
- ¼ cup heavy cream
- ¼ cup grated parmesan cheese
- 200 grams zucchini

Instructions

1. Heat the oil in a large skillet over medium-high heat.
2. Season the chicken with salt and pepper to taste, then add to the skillet.
3. Cook for 6 to 7 minutes on each side until cooked through, then slice into strips.
4. Reheat the skillet over medium-low heat and add the butter.
5. Stir in the heavy cream and parmesan cheese, then cook until thickened.
6. Spiralize the zucchini, then toss it into the sauce mixture with the chicken.
7. Cook until the zucchini is tender, about 2 minutes, then serve hot.

Nutrition info:
Calories: 595 Fat: 40 g Protein: 55 g Total Carbs: 4 g Fiber: 1 g Net Carbs: 3 g

Lunch recipes

Easy Cloud buns

Prep Time: 10 minutes
Cook Time: 30 minutes
Servings: 10

Ingredients

- Three large eggs, separated
- 1/8 teaspoon cream of tartar
- 3 ounces cream cheese, chopped

Instructions

1. Preheat the oven to 300°F and line a baking sheet with parchment.
2. Beat the egg whites until foamy, then beat in the cream of tartar until the whites are shiny and opaque with soft peaks.
3. In a separate bowl, beat the cream cheese and egg yolks until well combined, then fold in the egg white mixture.
4. Spoon the batter onto the baking sheet in ¼-cup circles about 2 inches apart.
5. Bake for 30 minutes until the buns are firm to the touch.

Nutrition info:

Calories: 50 Fat: 4.5 g Protein: 2.5 g Total Carbs: 0.5 g Fiber: 0 g Net Carbs: 0.5 g

Lunch recipes

Baked chicken nuggets

Prep time: 10 minutes
 Cook time: 20 minutes
Servings: 4

Ingredients:

- ¼ cup almond flour
- One teaspoon chili powder
- ½ teaspoon paprika
- 2 pounds boneless chicken thighs, cut into 2-inch chunks
- Salt and pepper
- Two large eggs whisked well

Instructions:

1. Preheat the oven to 400°f and line a baking sheet with parchment.
2. Stir together the almond flour, chili powder, and paprika in a shallow dish.
3. Season the chicken with salt and pepper, then dip in the beaten eggs.
4. Dredge the chicken pieces in the almond flour mixture, then arrange on the baking sheet.
5. Bake for 20 minutes until browned and crisp. Serve hot.

Nutrition info:

400 calories, 26g fat, 43g protein, 2g carbs, 1g fiber, 1g net carbs

Lunch recipes

Three-cheese pizza frittata

Prep Time: 10 minutes
Cook Time: 40 minutes
Servings: 4

Ingredients

- ½ (10-ounce) bag frozen spinach, thawed
- Six large eggs
- Two tablespoons olive oil
- ½ teaspoon dried Italian seasoning
- Salt and pepper
- ¼ cup ricotta cheese
- ¼ cup grated parmesan cheese
- 2 ½ ounces shredded mozzarella cheese
- 1 ounce sliced pepperoni

Instructions

1. Preheat the oven to 375°F and grease a pie plate with cooking spray.
2. Defrost the frozen spinach in the microwave for 4 minutes, then squeeze out the water.
3. Whisk together the eggs, olive oil, Italian seasoning, salt, and pepper in a bowl.
4. Stir in the ricotta cheese, parmesan cheese, and drained spinach until well combined.
5. Pour the mixture into the pie plate and top with mozzarella and pepperoni.
6. Bake for 35 to 40 minutes until the egg is set and the cheese lightly browned.

Nutrition info:
Calories: 305 Fat: 24 g Protein: 21 g Total Carbs: 3.5 g Fiber: 1 g Net Carbs: 2.5 g

Lunch recipes

Egg salad over lettuce

Prep time: 10 minutes
Cook time: none
Servings: 2

Ingredients:

- Three large hardboiled eggs cooled
- One small stalk celery, diced
- Three tablespoons mayonnaise
- One tablespoon fresh chopped parsley

- One teaspoon fresh lemon juice
- Salt and pepper
- 4 cups fresh chopped lettuce

Instructions:

1. Peel and dice the eggs into a mixing bowl.
2. Stir in the celery, mayonnaise, parsley, lemon juice, salt, and pepper.
3. Serve spooned over fresh chopped lettuce.

Nutrition info:

260 calories, 23g fat, 10g protein, 4g carbs, 1g fiber, 3g net carbs

Lunch recipes

Mozzarella tuna melt

Prep Time: 10 minutes
Cook Time: 10 minutes
Servings: 4

Ingredients

- One tablespoon olive oil
- ½ cup diced yellow onion
- 8 ounces of canned tuna
- ¼ cup mayonnaise
- Four large eggs whisked
- 2 ounces shredded mozzarella cheese
- Salt and pepper
- One green onion, sliced thin

Instructions

1. Heat the oil in a skillet over medium heat.
2. Add the onion and cook until translucent, about 5 minutes.
3. Drain the tuna, then flake it into the skillet and stir in the remaining ingredients.
4. Season with salt and pepper and cook for 2 minutes or until the cheese melts.
5. Spoon into a bowl and top with sliced green onion to serve.

Nutrition info:

Calories: 550 Fat: 36 g Protein: 45 g Total Carbs: 11.5 g Fiber: 1 g Net Carbs: 10.5 g

Lunch recipes

Cheesy Single-serve lasagna

Prep Time: 15 minutes
Cook Time: 5 minutes
Servings: 2

Ingredients

- Three tablespoons low-carb marinara sauce
- One small zucchini (60g), sliced very thin into rounds
- Two tablespoons ricotta cheese
- 3 ounces shredded mozzarella
- Dried oregano

Instructions

1. Spoon one tablespoon marinara sauce into a microwave-safe bowl.
2. Spread one-third of the zucchini slices over the sauce then cover with a tablespoon of ricotta.
3. Repeat the layers of sauce, zucchini, and ricotta.
4. Top with the remaining zucchini and the last tablespoon of marinara.
5. Sprinkle with mozzarella, then microwave for 3 to 4 minutes until the entire mixture is heated through and the cheese is melted.
6. Sprinkle with dried oregano and serve hot.

Nutrition info:
Calories: 325 Fat: 19 g Protein: 29 g Total Carbs: 10 g Fiber: 1.5 g Net Carbs: 8.5 g

Lunch recipes

Fried salmon cakes

Prep time: 15 minutes
Cook time: 10 minutes
Servings: 2

Ingredients:

- One tablespoon butter
- 1 cup riced cauliflower
- Salt and pepper
- 8 ounces boneless salmon fillet
- ¼ cup almond flour
- Two tablespoons coconut flour

- One large egg
- Two tablespoons minced red onion
- One tablespoon fresh chopped parsley
- Two tablespoons coconut oil

Instructions:

1. Melt the butter in a skillet over medium heat, then cook the cauliflower for 5 minutes until tender – season with salt and pepper.
2. Spoon the cauliflower into a bowl and reheat the skillet.
3. Add the salmon and season with salt and pepper.
4. Cook the salmon until just opaque, then remove and flake the fish into a bowl.
5. Stir in the cauliflower along with the almond flour, coconut flour, egg, red onion, and parsley.
6. Shape into six patties, then fries in coconut oil until both sides browned.

Nutrition info:
505 calories, 37.5g fat, 31g protein, 14.5g carbs, 8g fiber, 6.5g net carbs

Lunch recipes

Crispy chipotle chicken thighs

Prep Time: 15 minutes
Cook Time: 15 minutes
Servings: 2

Ingredients

- ½ teaspoon chipotle chili powder
- ¼ teaspoon garlic powder
- ¼ teaspoon onion powder
- ¼ teaspoon ground coriander
- ¼ teaspoon smoked paprika
- 12 ounces boneless chicken thighs
- Salt and pepper
- One tablespoon olive oil
- 3 cups fresh baby spinach

Instructions

1. Combine the chipotle chili powder, garlic powder, onion powder, coriander, and smoked paprika in a small bowl.
2. Pound the chicken thighs out flat then season with salt and pepper on both sides.
3. Cut the chicken thighs in half and heat the oil in a heavy skillet over medium-high heat.
4. Add the chicken thighs skin-side-down to the skillet and sprinkle with the spice mixture.

5. Cook the chicken thighs for 8 minutes, then flip and cook on the other side for 3 to 5 minutes.
6. During the last 3 minutes, add the spinach to the skillet and cook until wilted.
7. Serve the crispy chicken thighs on a bed of wilted spinach.

Nutrition info:
Calories: 400 Fat: 20 g Protein: 51 g Total Carbs: 3 g Fiber: 1.5 g Net Carbs: 1.5 g

Lunch recipes

Sesame chicken avocado salad

Prep time: 10 minutes
Cook time: none
Servings: 2

Ingredients:

- One tablespoon sesame oil
- 8 ounces boneless chicken thighs, chopped
- Salt and pepper
- 4 cups fresh spring greens
- 1 cup sliced avocado
- Two tablespoons olive oil
- Two tablespoons of rice wine vinegar
- One tablespoon sesame seeds

Instructions:

1. Heat the sesame oil in a skillet over medium-high heat.
2. Season the chicken with salt and pepper, then add to the skillet.
3. Cook the chicken until browned and cooked through, stirring often.
4. Remove the chicken from the heat and cool slightly.
5. Divide the spring greens onto two salad plates and top with avocado.
6. Drizzle the salads with olive oil and rice wine vinegar.
7. Top with cooked chicken and sprinkle with sesame seeds to serve.

Nutrition info:
540 calories, 47.5g fat, 23g protein, 10.5g carbs, 8g fiber, 2.5g net carbs

Lunch recipes

Pepperoni, Ham & Cheddar Stromboli

Prep Time: 20 minutes
Cook Time: 20 minutes
Servings: 3

Ingredients

- One ¼ cups shredded mozzarella cheese
- ¼ cup almond flour
- Three tablespoons coconut flour
- One teaspoon dried Italian seasoning
- Salt and pepper
- One large egg whisked
- 6 ounces sliced deli ham
- 2 ounces sliced pepperoni
- 4 ounces shredded cheddar cheese
- One tablespoon melted butter
- 6 cups fresh salad greens

Instructions

Preheat the oven to 400°F and line a baking sheet with parchment.
Melt the mozzarella cheese in a microwave-safe bowl until it can be stirred smooth.
In a separate bowl, stir together the almond flour, coconut flour, and dried Italian seasoning.
Pour the melted cheese into the flour mixture and work it together with some salt and pepper.
Add the egg and work it into a dough, then turn out onto a piece of parchment.
Lay a piece of parchment on top and roll the dough out into an oval.
Use a knife to cut diagonal slits along the edges, leaving the middle 4 inches untouched.
Layer the ham and cheese slices in the middle of the dough then fold the strips over the top.
Brush the top with butter then bake for 15 to 20 minutes until the dough is browned.
Slice the Stromboli and serve with a small salad.

Nutrition info:
Calories: 525 Fat: 37 g Protein: 32 g Total Carbs: 16 g Fiber: 8 g Net Carbs: 8 g

Lunch recipes

Cheesy Buffalo chicken sandwich

Prep time: 10 minutes
Cook time: 20
Servings: 1
Ingredients:

- One large egg, separated into white and yolk
- Pinch cream of tartar
- Pinch salt
- 1-ounce cream cheese softened
- 1 cup cooked chicken breast, shredded
- Two tablespoons hot sauce
- One slice swiss cheese

Instructions:

1. For the bread, preheat the oven to 300°f and line a baking sheet with parchment.
2. Beat the egg whites with the cream of tartar and salt until soft peaks form.
3. Whisk the cream cheese and egg yolk until smooth and pale yellow.
4. Fold in the egg whites a little at a time until smooth and well combined.
5. Spoon the batter onto the baking sheet into two even circles.
6. Bake for 25 minutes until firm and lightly browned.
7. Shred the chicken into a bowl and toss with the hot sauce.
8. Spoon the chicken onto one of the bread circles and top with cheese.
9. Top with the other bread circle and enjoy it.

Nutrition info:
555 calories, 33.5g fat, 58g protein, 3.5g carbs, 0g fiber, 3.5g net carbs

Lunch recipes

Spring Salad with Steak & sweet dressing

Prep Time: 10 minutes
Cook Time: 25 minutes
Servings: 4

Ingredients

- Two slices thick-cut bacon
- Two tablespoons white wine vinegar
- Two tablespoons olive oil
- Two tablespoons fresh raspberries
- Liquid stevia, to taste
- 4 cups fresh spring greens
- 1-ounce toasted pine nuts
- One tablespoon butter
- 7 ounces beef flank steak

Instructions
1. Cook the bacon in a skillet over medium-high heat until very crisp, then chop fine.

2. Combine the white wine vinegar, olive oil, raspberries, and liquid stevia in a blender.
3. Blend the ingredients until smooth and well combined.
4. Combine the spring greens, roasted pine nuts, and crumbled bacon in a large bowl.
5. Toss with the dressing then divide between two plates.
6. Melt the butter in a heavy skillet over medium-high heat, then add the steak.
7. Season with salt and pepper then sear on one side, about 3 to 4 minutes.
8. Flip the steak and cook to the desired level, then rest for 5 minutes.

Nutrition info:
Calories: 575 Fat: 43.5 g Protein: 41 g Total Carbs: 6.5 g Fiber: 4 g Net Carbs: 2.5 g

Lunch recipes

Avocado spinach salad with almonds

Prep time: 10 minutes
Cook time: none
Servings: 2

Ingredients:

- 4 cups fresh baby spinach
- Two tablespoons olive oil
- 1 ½ tablespoon balsamic vinegar
- ½ tablespoon dijon mustard
- Salt and pepper
- One medium avocado, sliced thinly
- ¼ cup sliced almonds, toasted

Instructions:

1. Toss the spinach with the olive oil, balsamic vinegar, dijon mustard, salt, and pepper.
2. Divide the spinach between two salad plates.
3. Top the salads with sliced avocado and toasted almonds to serve.

Nutrition info:
415 calories, 40g fat, 6.5g protein, 14g carbs, 10g fiber, 4g net carbs

Lunch recipes

Cabbage and Sausage skillet

Prep Time: 10 minutes
Cook Time: 20 minutes
Servings: 4

Ingredients

- Six extensive Italian sausage links
- ½ head green cabbage, sliced
- Two tablespoons butter
- ¼ cup sour cream
- ¼ cup mayonnaise
- Salt and pepper

Instructions

1. Cook the sausage in a skillet over medium-high heat until evenly browned, then slice them.
2. Reheat the skillet over medium-high heat then add the butter.
3. Toss in the cabbage and cook until wilted, about 3 to 4 minutes.
4. Stir the sliced sausage into the cabbage, then stir in the sour cream and mayonnaise.
5. Season with salt and pepper, then simmer for 10 minutes.

Nutrition info:
Calories: 350 Fat: 24.5 g Protein: 22 g Total Carbs: 12 g Fiber: 2 g Net Carbs: 10 g

Lunch recipes

Cauliflower leek soup with pancetta

Prep time: 15 minutes
Cook time: 1 hour
Servings: 4

Ingredients:

- 4 cups chicken broth
- ½ medium head cauliflower, chopped
- 1 cup sliced leeks
- ½ cup heavy cream
- Salt and pepper

- 2 ounces diced pancetta

Instructions:

1. Combine the broth and cauliflower in a saucepan over medium-high heat.
2. Bring the chicken broth to a boil then add the sliced leeks.
3. Boil on medium heat, covered, for 1 hour until the cauliflower is tender.
4. Remove from heat and puree the soup with an immersion blender.
5. Stir in the cream, then season with salt and pepper.
6. Fry the chopped pancetta in a skillet over medium-high heat until crisp.
7. Spoon the soup into bowls and sprinkle with pancetta to serve.

Nutrition info:
200 calories, 13g fat, 12g protein, 8.5g carbs, 2g fiber, 6.5g net carbs

Lunch recipes

Mozzarella Veggie-loaded quiche

Prep Time: 10 minutes
Cook Time: 25 minutes
Servings: 4

Ingredients

- Six tablespoons almond flour
- One tablespoon grated parmesan cheese
- Four large eggs, divided
- Two slices thick-cut bacon
- ¼ cup frozen spinach, thawed and drained well
- ¼ cup diced zucchini
- ¼ cup shredded mozzarella cheese
- Four cherry tomatoes halved
- One tablespoon heavy cream
- One teaspoon chopped chives

Instructions

1. Stir together the almond flour and grated parmesan with one egg and a pinch of salt until it forms a soft dough.
2. Press the dough into the bottom of a small quiche pan as evenly as possible.
3. Score the bottom and sides of the dough, then bake for 7 minutes at 325°F and let cool.
4. Cook the bacon in a skillet until browned, then crumble and spread in the quiche pan.
5. Sprinkle in the spinach, zucchini, cheese, and tomatoes.
6. Whisk together the remaining egg with the heavy cream, chives, salt, and pepper, then pour into the quiche. Bake for 22 to 25 minutes until the egg is set, then serve hot.

Nutrition info:
Calories: 590 Fat: 40 g Protein: 38 g Total Carbs: 24.5 g Fiber: 7.5 g Net Carbs: 17 g

Lunch recipes

Beef and pepper kebabs

Prep time: 30 minutes
Cook time: 10 minutes
Servings: 2

Ingredients:

- Two tablespoons olive oil
- 1 ½ tablespoon balsamic vinegar
- Two teaspoons Dijon mustard
- Salt and pepper
- 8 ounces beef sirloin, cut into 2-inch pieces
- One small red pepper, cut into chunks
- One little green pepper, cut into chunks

Instructions:

1. Whisk together the olive oil, balsamic vinegar, and mustard in a shallow dish.
2. Season the steak with salt and pepper, then toss in the marinade.
3. Let marinate for 30 minutes, then slide onto skewers with the peppers.
4. Preheat a grill pan to high heat and grease with cooking spray.
5. Cook the kebabs for 2 to 3 minutes on each side until the beef is done.

Nutrition info:
365 calories, 21.5g fat, 35.5g protein, 6.5g carbs, 1.5g fiber, 5g net carbs

Lunch recipes

Savory ham and cheese waffles

Prep Time: 15 minutes
Cook Time: 25 minutes
Servings: 2

Ingredients

- Four large eggs, divided

- Two scoops (40g) egg white protein powder
- One teaspoon baking powder
- 1/3 cup melted butter
- ½ teaspoon salt
- 1-ounce diced ham
- ¼ cup shredded cheddar cheese

Instructions

1. Separate two of the eggs and set the other two aside.
2. Beat 2 of the egg yolks with the protein powder, baking powder, butter, and salt in a mixing bowl.
3. Fold in the chopped ham and grated cheddar cheese.
4. Whisk the egg whites in a separate bowl with a pinch of salt until stiff peaks form.
5. Fold the beaten egg whites into the egg yolk mixture in two batches.
6. Grease a preheated waffle maker, then spoon ¼ cup of the batter into it and close it.
7. Cook until the waffle is golden brown, about 3 to 4 minutes, then remove.
8. Reheat the waffle iron and repeat with the remaining batter.
9. Meanwhile, heat the oil in a skillet and fry the eggs with salt and pepper.
10. Serve the waffles hot, topped with a fried egg.

Nutrition info:
Calories: 575 Fat: 46.5 g Protein: 35 g Total Carbs: 5 g Fiber: 0 g Net Carbs: 5 g

Lunch recipes

Egg, and cheese sandwich

Prep time: 30 minutes
Cook time: 5 minutes
Servings: 1

Ingredients:

- One large egg, separated
- Pinch cream of tartar
- Pinch salt
- 1-ounce cream cheese softened
- One large egg
- One teaspoon butter
- 3 ounces sliced ham
- One slice cheddar cheese

Instructions:

1. For the bread, preheat the oven to 300°f and line a baking sheet with parchment.

2. Beat the egg whites with the cream of tartar and salt until soft peaks form.
3. Whisk the cream cheese and egg yolk until smooth and pale yellow.
4. Fold in the egg whites a little at a time until smooth and well combined.
5. Spoon the batter onto the baking sheet into two even circles.
6. Bake for 25 minutes until firm and lightly browned.
7. To complete the sandwich, fry the egg in butter until done to your preference.
8. Arrange the sliced ham on top of one bread circle.
9. Top with the fried egg and the sliced cheese, then the second bread circle.
10. Serve immediately or cook in a greased skillet to melt the cheese first.

Nutrition info:
530 calories, 40g fat, 36g protein, 5.5g carbs, 1g fiber, 4.5g net carbs

Lunch recipes

Bacon-wrapped hot dogs

Prep time: 10 minutes
Cook time: 30 minutes
Servings: 2

Ingredients:

- Four all-beef hot dogs
- Two slices cheddar cheese
- Four slices uncooked bacon

Instructions:

1. Slice the hotdogs lengthwise, cutting halfway through the thickness.
2. Cut the cheese slices in half and stuff one half into each hot dog.
3. Wrap the hotdogs in bacon then place them on a foil-lined roasting pan.
4. Bake for 30 minutes or until the bacon is crisp.

Nutrition info:
500 calories, 43g fat, 24g protein, 4g carbs, 0g fiber, 4g net carbs

Lunch recipes

Fat-Busting Vanilla Protein Smoothie

Prep Time: 5 minutes
Cook Time: none
Servings: 2

Ingredients

- One scoop (20g) vanilla egg white protein powder
- ½ cup heavy cream
- ¼ cup vanilla almond milk
- Four ice cubes
- One tablespoon coconut oil
- One tablespoon powdered erythritol
- ½ teaspoon vanilla extract
- ¼ cup whipped cream

Instructions

1. Combine all of the ingredients except the whipped cream in a blender.
2. Blend on high speed for 30 to 60 seconds until smooth.
3. Pour into a glass and top with whipped cream.

Nutrition info:

Calories: 540 Fat: 46 g Protein: 25 g Total Carbs: 8 g Fiber: 0.5 g Net Carbs: 7.5 g

Lunch recipes

Curried chicken soup

Prep time: 10 minutes
Cook time: 20 minutes
Servings: 4

Ingredients:

- Two tablespoons olive oil, divided
- Four boneless chicken thighs (about 12 ounces)
- One small yellow onion, chopped
- Two teaspoons curry powder
- Two teaspoons ground cumin
- Pinch cayenne
- 4 cups chopped cauliflower
- 4 cups chicken broth
- 1 cup of water
- Two cloves minced garlic
- ½ cup of canned coconut milk
- 2 cups chopped kale
- Fresh chopped cilantro

Instructions:

1. Chop the chicken into bite-sized pieces then set aside.
2. Heat 1 tablespoon oil in a saucepan over medium heat.
3. Add the onions and cook for 4 minutes then stir in half of the spices.
4. Stir in the cauliflower and sauté for another 4 minutes.
5. Pour in the broth, then add the water and garlic and bring to a boil.
6. Reduce heat and simmer for 10 minutes until the cauliflower softened.
7. Remove from heat and stir in the coconut milk and kale.
8. Heat the remaining oil in a skillet and add the chicken – cook until browned.
9. Stir in the rest of the spices then cook until the chicken is done.
10. Stir the chicken into the soup and serve hot, garnished with fresh cilantro.

Nutrition info:

390 calories, 22g fat, 34g protein, 14.5g carbs, 4.5g fiber, 10g net carbs

Lunch recipes

Lamb Chops with Rosemary and Garlic

Prep Time: 35 minutes
Cook Time: 15 minutes
Servings: 4

Ingredients

- One tablespoon coconut oil, melted
- One teaspoon fresh chopped rosemary
- One clove garlic, minced
- Two bone-in lamb chops (about 6 ounces meat)
- One tablespoon butter
- Salt and pepper
- ¼ pound fresh asparagus, trimmed
- One tablespoon olive oil

Instructions

1. Combine the coconut oil, rosemary, and garlic in a shallow dish.
2. Add the lamb chops then turn to coat – let marinate in the fridge overnight.
3. Let the lamb rest at room temperature for 30 minutes.
4. Heat the butter in a large skillet over medium-high heat.
5. Add the lamb chops and cook for 6 minutes, then season with salt and pepper.
6. Turn the chops and cook for another 6 minutes or until cooked to the desired level.
7. Let the lamb chops rest for 5 minutes before serving.
8. Meanwhile, toss the asparagus with olive oil, salt, and pepper then spread on a baking sheet.
9. Broil for 6 to 8 minutes until charred, shaking occasionally. Serve hot with the lamb chops.

Lunch recipes

Cheesy Sausage and Mushroom Skillet

Prep Time: 15 minutes
Cook Time: 15 minutes
Servings: 4

Ingredients

- One tablespoon coconut oil
- 6 ounces Italian sausage, crumbled
- 4 ounces sliced mushrooms
- One small yellow onion, chopped
- ½ teaspoon dried oregano
- ¼ teaspoon dried thyme
- Salt and pepper
- ¼ cup marinara sauce
- ¼ cup of water
- ½ cup shredded mozzarella cheese

Instructions

1. Preheat the oven to 350°F.
2. Heat the oil in a large cast-iron skillet over medium heat until smoking.
3. Add the sausages and cook until browned and almost cooked through.
4. Remove the sausages to a cutting board and let cool for a few minutes.
5. Add the mushroom and onion to the skillet and cook for 3 to 4 minutes until browned.
6. Slice the sausages and add them back to the skillet.
7. Stir in the oregano, thyme, salt, and pepper.
8. Pour in the sauce and water, then stir well. Transfer the skillet to the oven and cook for 10 minutes.
9. Sprinkle with mozzarella then cook another 5 minutes until melted.

Nutrition info:
Calories: 630 Fat: 48 g Protein: 33 g Total Carbs: 11 g Fiber: 2 g Net Carbs: 9 g

Lunch recipes

Chicken enchilada soup

Prep time: 15 minutes
Cook time: 45 minutes
Servings: 4

Ingredients:

- Two tablespoons coconut oil
- Two medium stalks celery, sliced
- One small yellow onion, chopped
- One little red pepper, chopped
- Two cloves garlic, minced
- 1 cup diced tomatoes
- Two teaspoons ground cumin
- One teaspoon chili powder
- ½ teaspoon dried oregano
- 4 cups chicken broth
- 1 cup of canned coconut milk
- 8 ounces cooked chicken thighs, chopped
- Two tablespoons fresh lime juice
- ¼ cup fresh chopped cilantro

Instructions:

1. Heat the oil in a saucepan over medium-high heat then add the celery, onion, peppers, and garlic – sauté for 4 to 5 minutes.
2. Stir in the garlic and cook for a minute until fragrant.
3. Add the tomatoes and spices, then cook for 3 minutes, stirring often.
4. Add the broth and bring the soup to a boil, then reduce heat and simmer for about 20 minutes.
5. Stir in the coconut milk and simmer for another 20 minutes, then add the chicken.
6. Cook until the chicken is heated through, then stir in the lime juice and cilantro.

Nutrition info:
380 calories, 27g fat, 24g protein, 12g carbs, 3.5g fiber, 8.5g net carbs

Lunch recipes

Rosemary roasted chicken and veggies

Prep Time: 15 minutes
Cook Time: 35 minutes
Servings: 2

Ingredients

- Four deboned chicken thighs
- Salt and pepper
- One small zucchini, sliced
- Two small carrots, peeled and sliced
- One small parsnip, peeled and sliced
- Two cloves garlic, sliced
- Three tablespoons olive oil
- One tablespoon balsamic vinegar
- Two teaspoons fresh chopped rosemary

Instructions

1. Preheat the oven to 350°F and lightly grease a small rimmed baking sheet with cooking spray.
2. Place the chicken thighs on the baking sheet and season with salt and pepper.
3. Arrange the veggies around the chicken then sprinkle with sliced garlic.
4. Whisk together the remaining ingredients, then drizzle over the chicken and veggies.
5. Bake for 30 minutes, then broil for 3 to 5 minutes until the skins are crisp.

Nutrition info:
Calories: 540 Fat: 40.5 g Protein: 33 g Total Carbs: 12 g Fiber: 3.5 g Net Carbs: 8.5 g

Lunch recipes

Mushroom and asparagus soup

Prep time: 10 minutes
Cook time: 30 minutes
Servings: 4

Ingredients:

- One tablespoon butter
- One small yellow onion, chopped
- Three cloves garlic, minced

- 1-pound asparagus, trimmed and chopped
- 2 cups sliced mushrooms
- 4 cups vegetable broth
- 4 cups fresh baby spinach
- One teaspoon fresh chopped tarragon
- ½ cup heavy cream
- ¼ cup fresh lemon juice
- ¼ cup fresh chopped parsley
- Salt and pepper

Instructions:

1. Melt the butter in a stockpot and add the onion.
2. Sauté the onion until browned, then stir in the garlic and cook 1 minute more.
3. Stir in the asparagus and mushrooms, then sauté for 4 minutes.
4. Pour in the vegetable broth along with the spinach and tarragon.
5. Bring to a boil, then reduce heat and simmer for 30 minutes on medium-low heat.
6. Remove from heat, then stir in the cream, lemon juice, and parsley.
7. Cover and let rest for 20 minutes, then season with salt and pepper to taste.

Nutrition info:
170 calories, 10.5g fat, 10g protein, 11g carbs, 4g fiber, 7g net carbs

Lunch recipes

Avocado lime salmon

Prep Time: 15 minutes
Cook Time: 15 minutes
Servings: 2

Ingredients

- 100 grams chopped cauliflower
- One large avocado
- One tablespoon fresh lime juice
- Two tablespoons diced red onion
- Two tablespoons olive oil
- 2 (6-ounce) boneless salmon fillets
- Salt and pepper

Instructions

1. Place the cauliflower in a food processor and pulse into rice-like grains.
2. Grease a skillet with cooking spray and heat over medium heat.

3. Add the cauliflower rice and cook, covered, for 8 minutes until tender. Set aside.
4. Combine the avocado, lime juice, and red onion in a food processor and blend smooth.
5. Heat the oil in a large skillet over medium-high heat.
6. Season the salmon with salt and pepper then add to the skillet skin-side down.
7. Cook for 4 to 5 minutes until seared, then flip and cook for another 4 to 5 minutes.
8. Serve the salmon over a bed of cauliflower rice topped with the avocado cream.

Nutrition info:

Calories: 570 Fat: 44 g Protein: 36 g Total Carbs: 12g Fiber: 8 g Net Carbs: 4 g

Lunch recipes

Easy Beef Curry

Prep Time: 20 minutes
Cook Time: 40 minutes
Servings: 4

Ingredients

- One medium yellow onion, chopped
- One tablespoon minced garlic
- One tablespoon grated ginger
- One ¼ cups canned coconut milk
- 1-pound beef chuck, chopped
- Two tablespoons curry powder
- One teaspoon salt
- ½ cup fresh chopped cilantro

Instructions

1. Combine the onion, garlic, and ginger in a food processor and blend into a paste.
2. Transfer the pasta to a saucepan and cook for 3 minutes on medium heat.
3. Stir in the coconut milk, then simmer gently for 10 minutes.
4. Add the chopped beef along with the curry powder and salt.
5. Stir well then simmer, covered, for 20 minutes.
6. Remove the lid and simmer for another 20 minutes until the beef is cooked through.
7. Adjust seasoning to taste and garnish with fresh chopped cilantro.

Nutrition info:

Calories: 550 Fat: 34 g Protein: 50 g Total Carbs: 14 g Fiber: 5 g Net Carbs: 9 g

Lunch recipes

Bacon-wrapped chicken rolls

Prep time: 5 minutes
Cook time: 35 minutes
Servings: 2

Ingredients:

- Six boneless, skinless, chicken breast halves
- Six slices uncooked bacon

Instructions:

1. Preheat the oven to 350°f.
2. Pound the chicken breast halves with a meat mallet to flatten.
3. Roll the chicken breast halves up then wrap each one with bacon.
4. Place the rolls on a foil-lined baking sheet.
5. Bake for 30 to 35 minutes until the chicken is done and the bacon crisp.

Nutrition info:
350 calories, 16g fat, 46g protein, 0.5g carbs, 0g fiber, 0.5g net carbs

Lunch recipes

Spicy shrimp and sausage soup

Prep time: 15 minutes
Cook time: 30 minutes
Servings: 4

Ingredients:

- One tablespoon olive oil
- Three small stalks celery, diced
- One small yellow onion, chopped
- One little red pepper, chopped
- Three cloves garlic, minced
- One tablespoon tomato paste
- Two teaspoons smoked paprika
- ½ teaspoon ground coriander
- Salt and pepper
- 8 ounces chorizo sausage, diced

- 1 cup diced tomatoes
- 4 cups chicken broth
- 12 ounces shrimp, peeled and deveined
- Fresh chopped cilantro

Instructions:

1. Heat the oil in a heavy stockpot over medium-high heat.
2. Add the celery, onion, and red pepper, and sauté for 6 to 8 minutes until tender.
3. Stir in the garlic, tomato paste, and seasonings, then cook for 1 minute.
4. Add the sausage and tomatoes and cook for 5 minutes.
5. Stir in the broth, then bring to a simmer and cook, uncovered, for 20 minutes.
6. Adjust seasoning to taste, then add the shrimp.
7. Simmer until just cooked through, about 3 to 4 minutes.
8. Spoon into bowls and serve with fresh cilantro.

Nutrition info:
465 calories, 28.5g fat, 39g protein, 11.5g carbs, 2g fiber, 9.5g net carbs

Lunch recipes

Spiced pumpkin soup

Prep Time: 15 minutes
Cook Time: 40 minutes
Servings: 3

Ingredients

- Two tablespoons unsalted butter
- One small yellow onion, chopped
- Two cloves minced garlic
- One teaspoon minced ginger
- ½ teaspoon ground cinnamon
- ¼ teaspoon ground nutmeg
- Salt and pepper to taste
- ½ cup pumpkin puree
- 1 cup chicken broth
- Three slices thick-cut bacon
- ¼ cup heavy cream

Instructions

1. Melt the butter in a large saucepan over medium heat.

2. Add the onions, garlic, and ginger and cook for 3 to 4 minutes until the onions are translucent.
3. Stir in the spices and cook for 1 minute until fragrant—season with salt and pepper.
4. Add the pumpkin puree and chicken broth, then bring to a boil.
5. Reduce heat and simmer for 20 minutes then remove from heat.
6. Puree the soup using an immersion blender then return to heat and simmer for 20 minutes.
7. Cook the bacon in a skillet until crisp, then remove paper towels to drain.
8. Add the bacon fat to the soup along with the heavy cream. Crumbled the bacon over the top to serve.

Nutrition info:
Calories: 250 Fat: 20 g Protein: 10 g Total Carbs: 8 g Fiber: 2 g Net Carbs: 6 g

Dinner recipes

Grilled pesto salmon with asparagus

Prep time: 5 minutes
Cook time: 15 minutes
Servings: 4

Ingredients:

- 4 (6-ounce) boneless salmon fillets
- Salt and pepper
- One bunch asparagus ends trimmed
- Two tablespoons olive oil
- ¼ cup basil pesto

Instructions:

1. Preheat a grill to high heat and oil the grates.
2. Season the salmon with salt and pepper, then spray with cooking spray.
3. Grill the salmon for 4 to 5 minutes on each side until cooked through
4. Toss the asparagus with oil and grill until tender, about 10 minutes.
5. Spoon the pesto over the salmon and serve with the asparagus.

Nutrition info:
300 calories, 17.5g fat, 34.5g protein, 2.5g carbs, 1.5g fiber, 1g net carbs

Dinner recipes

Super Packed Cheese Omelets

Prep Time: 5 min
Cook Time: 10 min
Servings: 1 servings

Ingredients:

- Three large mushrooms sliced.
- Three large eggs.
- 1 oz cheddar cheese grated.
- 1 oz butter.
- ¼ onion finely sliced.
- Pinch salt and Pepper.

Instructions:

1. In a bowl, whisk together the eggs, salt, and Pepper.
2. In a large frying pan, melt the butter and fry onions and mushrooms until tender. Pour in the egg mixture so that it surrounds the onions and mushrooms.
3. As the sides begin to firm and it is still slightly runny in the middle, sprinkle on the cheese.
4. Continue cooking until the egg mixture is completely formed and cooked.

Nutrition info:
Fat: 43g, Carbohydrates: 5g, Protein: 24g, Calories: 511

Dinner recipes

Sweet Blueberry coconut porridge

Prep Time: 5 minutes
Cook Time: 15 minutes
Servings: 2

Ingredients

- 1 cup unsweetened almond milk
- ¼ cup canned coconut milk
- ¼ cup coconut flour
- ¼ cup ground flaxseed
- One teaspoon ground cinnamon

- ¼ teaspoon ground nutmeg
- Pinch salt
- 60 grams fresh blueberries
- ¼ cup shaved coconut

Instructions

1. Warm the almond milk and coconut milk in a saucepan over low heat.
2. Whisk in the coconut flour, flaxseed, cinnamon, nutmeg, and salt.
3. Turn up the heat and cook until the mixture bubbles.
4. Stir in the sweetener and vanilla extract, then cook until thickened to the desired level.
5. Spoon into two bowls and top with blueberries and shaved coconut.

Nutrition info:
Calories: 390 Fat: 22 g Protein: 10 g Total Carbs: 37 g Fiber: 22 g Net Carbs: 15 g

Dinner recipes

Simple Stay-at-home Spinach & Eggs

Prep Time: 10 min
Cook Time: 5 min
Servings: 1 servings

Ingredients:

- Two large eggs.
- ½ cup baby spinach.
- 2 tbsp mayonnaise.
- 1 tbsp butter.
- Pinch salt and Pepper.

Instructions:

1. Melt butter in a large frying pan and crack in the eggs.
2. As the eggs are frying, spoon over the melted butter from the pan until the yolk begins to have a white tint.
3. Place spinach on a plate with the mayonnaise, season with salt and Pepper; place eggs next to spinach.

Nutrition info:
Fat: 40g, Carbohydrates: 1g, Protein: 13g, Calories: 419

Dinner recipes

Rosemary roasted pork with cauliflower

Prep time: 10 minutes
Cook time: 20 minutes
Servings: 4

Ingredients:

- 1 ½ pound boneless pork tenderloin
- One tablespoon coconut oil
- One tablespoon fresh chopped rosemary
- Salt and pepper
- One tablespoon olive oil
- 2 cups cauliflower florets

Instructions:

1. Rub the pork with coconut oil, then season with rosemary, salt, and pepper.
2. Heat the olive oil in a large skillet over medium-high heat.
3. Add the pork and cook for 2 to 3 minutes on each side until browned.
4. Sprinkle the cauliflower in the skillet around the pork.
5. Reduce the heat to low, then cover the skillet and cook for 8 to 10 minutes until the pork is cooked through.
6. Slice the pork and serve with the cauliflower.

Nutrition info:
300 calories, 15.5g fat, 37g protein, 3g carbs, 1.5g fiber, 1.5g net carbs

Dinner recipes

Chewy Coconut Chunks

Prep Time: 10 min
Cook Time: 15 min
Servings: 8 servings
Ingredients:
- 7 oz coconut (shredded).
- ⅔ cup coconut milk (full fat).
- ¼ cup maple syrup.
- 1 tsp psyllium husk.
- ¼ tsp almond extract.
- ¼ tsp salt.

Instructions:

1. Preheat oven at 325 degrees.
2. In a blender, mix coconut milk, maple syrup, psyllium husk, almond extract, salt, and ¾ of the coconut flakes until smooth.
3. Pour mixture into a large bowl, stir in remaining coconut flakes.
4. Line a baking tray with greaseproof paper. Using a tablespoon, scoop out chunks of the mixture and place onto the plate.
5. Bake for 30 minutes or until all chunks are golden brown.

Nutrition info:

Fat: 10g, Carbohydrates: 7g, Protein: 2g, Calories: 111

Dinner recipes

Grilled salmon and zucchini with mango sauce

Prep time: 5 minutes
Cook time: 10 minutes
Servings: 4

Ingredients:

- 4 (6-ounce) boneless salmon fillets
- One tablespoon olive oil
- Salt and pepper
- One large zucchini, sliced in coins
- Two tablespoons fresh lemon juice
- ½ cup chopped mango
- ¼ cup fresh chopped cilantro
- One teaspoon lemon zest
- ½ cup of canned coconut milk

Instructions:

1. Preheat a grill pan to high heat and spray liberally with cooking spray.
2. Brush the salmon with olive oil and season with salt and pepper.
3. Toss the zucchini with lemon juice and season with salt and pepper.
4. Place the salmon fillets and zucchini on the grill pan.
5. Cook for 5 minutes, then turn everything and cook 5 minutes more.
6. Combine the remaining ingredients in a blender and blend into a sauce.
7. Serve the salmon fillets drizzled with the mango sauce and zucchini on the side.

Nutrition info:

350 calories, 21.5g fat, 35g protein, 8g carbs, 2g fiber, 6g net carbs

Dinner recipes

Craftily Creamy Chocolate Mousse

Prep Time: 5 min
Cook Time: 15 min
Servings: 2

Ingredients:

- 3 oz cream cheese.
- ½ cup of thick cream.
- ¼ cup powdered sweetener.
- 2 tbsp cocoa powder.
- 1 tsp vanilla extract.
- Pinch of salt.

Instructions:

1. In a blender, mix the cream cheese until soft and fluffy.
2. Slowly add in the thick cream, vanilla extract, sweetener, cocoa powder, and salt.
3. Mix until well blended and soft and fluffy.
4. Chill in the fridge for 30 minutes.

Nutrition info:

Fat: 38g, Carbohydrates: 6.5g, Protein: 7g, Calories: 372

Dinner recipes

Beef and broccoli stir-fry

Prep time: 20 minutes
Cook time: 15 minutes
Servings: 4

Ingredients:

- ¼ cup of soy sauce
- One tablespoon sesame oil
- One teaspoon garlic chili paste
- 1-pound beef sirloin
- Two tablespoons almond flour
- Two tablespoons coconut oil
- 2 cups chopped broccoli florets
- One tablespoon grated ginger
- Three cloves garlic, minced

Instructions:

1. Whisk together the soy sauce, sesame oil, and chili paste in a small bowl.
2. Slice the beef and toss with almond flour, then place in a plastic freezer bag.

3. Pour in the sauce and toss to coat, then let rest for 20 minutes.
4. Heat the oil in a large skillet over medium-high heat.
5. Pour the beef and sauce into the skillet and cook until the meat browned.
6. Push the beef to the sides of the skillet and add the broccoli, ginger, and garlic.
7. Sauté until the broccoli is tender-crisp, then toss it all together and serve hot.

Nutrition info:
350 calories, 19g fat, 37.5g protein, 6.5g carbs, 2g fiber, 4.5g net carbs

Dinner recipes

Peanut Butter Biscuits

Prep Time: 5 min
Cook Time: 15 min
Servings: 6 servings

Ingredients:
- 1 cup almond flour.
- ½ cup peanut butter (unsweetened).
- ⅓ cup erythritol.
- 1 tbsp coconut oil.
- ¾ tsp baking powder.
- ½ tsp vanilla extract.

Instructions:
1. Preheat oven at 350 degrees.
2. In a large bowl, mix all of the ingredients until a dough is formed.
3. Divide the dough into eight large biscuits.
4. Line a baking tray with greaseproof paper.
5. Bake for 10-12 minutes or until golden brown.

Nutrition info:
Fat:16g, Carbohydrates: 6g, Protein: 7g, Calories: 189

Dinner recipes

Hearty beef and bacon casserole

Prep time: 25 minutes
Cook time: 30 minutes
Servings: 8

Ingredients:

- Eight slices uncooked bacon

- One medium head cauliflower, chopped
- ¼ cup canned coconut milk
- Salt and pepper
- 2 pounds ground beef (80% lean)
- 8 ounces mushrooms, sliced
- One large yellow onion, chopped
- Two cloves garlic, minced

Instructions:

1. Preheat the oven to 375˚f.
2. Cook the bacon in a skillet until crisp, then drain on paper towels and chop.
3. Bring a pot of salted water to boil, then add the cauliflower.
4. Boil for 6 to 8 minutes until tender, then drain and add to a food processor with the coconut milk.
5. Blend the mixture until smooth, then season with salt and pepper.
6. Cook the beef in a skillet until browned, then drain the fat.
7. Stir in the mushrooms, onion, and garlic, then transfer to a baking dish.
8. Spread the cauliflower mixture over the top and bake for 30 minutes.
9. Broil on high heat for 5 minutes, then sprinkle with bacon to serve.

Nutrition info:
410 calories, 25.5g fat, 37g protein, 7.5g carbs, 3g fiber, 4.5g net carbs

Dinner recipes

Curiously Charming Keto Carrot Cake

Prep Time: 5 min
Cook Time: 15 min
Servings: 2

Ingredients:

- ¾ cup almond flour.
- ½ cup carrot (grated).
- One large egg.
- 2 tbsp cream cheese.
- 2 tbsp walnuts finely chopped.
- 2 tbsp butter melted.
- 2 tbsp erythritol.
- 1 tbsp thick cream.
- 2 tsp cinnamon.
- 1 tsp mixed spice.
- 1 tsp baking powder.

Instructions:

1. In a bowl, mix almond flour, cinnamon, baking powder, erythritol, walnuts, and mixed spice.
2. Mix in the egg, butter, thick cream, and carrot until well combined.
3. Grease 2 microwave-safe ramekins and split the mixture evenly between the two.
4. Microwave on high for 5 minutes.
5. Spread cream cheese on the top.

Nutrition info:

Fat: 40g, Carbohydrates: 5g, Protein: 14g, Calories: 443

Dinner recipes

Fried coconut shrimp with asparagus

Prep time: 15 minutes
Cook time: 10 minutes
Servings: 6

Ingredients:

- 1 ½ cups shredded unsweetened coconut
- Two large eggs
- Salt and pepper
- 1 ½ pound large shrimp, peeled and deveined

- ½ cup of canned coconut milk
- 1-pound asparagus, cut into 2-inch pieces

Instructions:

1. Pour the coconut into a shallow dish.
2. Beat the eggs with some salt and pepper in a bowl.
3. Dip the shrimp first in the egg, then dredge with coconut.
4. Heat the coconut oil in a large skillet over medium-high heat.
5. Add the shrimp and fry for 1 to 2 minutes on each side until browned.
6. Remove the shrimp to paper towels and reheat the skillet.
7. Add the asparagus and season with salt and pepper – sauté until tender-crisp, then serve with the shrimp.

Nutrition info:
535 calories, 38.5g fat, 29.5g protein, 18g carbs, 10g fiber, 8g net carbs

Dinner recipes

Almond & Vanilla Keto Cheesecake

Prep Time: 5 min
Cook Time: 10 min
Servings: 3 servings

Ingredients:

- 16 oz cream cheese.
- 2 cups almond flour.
- One ¼ cup erythritol.
- ¾ cup of thick cream.
- ½ cup sour cream.
- ⅓ cup of butter melted.
- 2 tsp vanilla extract.

Instructions:

1. Mix butter, flour, ¼ cup erythritol, and 1 tsp vanilla until a dough is formed.
2. Press the dough into a 9-inch ovenproof dish and chill for 60 minutes.
3. In a blender, mix cream cheese, 1 cup erythritol, and remaining vanilla until creamy.
4. Add in the sour cream and thick cream until thickened.
5. Pour onto chilled crust and refrigerate for 4-5 hours.

Nutritional Info:
Fat: 43g, Carbohydrates: 6g, Protein: 9g, Calories: 435

Dinner recipes

Spicy chicken enchilada casserole

Prep time: 15 minutes

Cook time: 1 hour

Servings: 6

Ingredients:

- 2 pounds boneless chicken thighs, chopped
- Salt and pepper
- 3 cups tomato salsa
- 1 ½ cups shredded cheddar cheese
- ¾ cup sour cream
- 1 cup diced avocado

Instructions:

1. Preheat the oven to 375°f and grease a casserole dish.
2. Season the chicken with salt and pepper then spread into the dish.
3. Spread the salsa over the chicken and sprinkle with cheese.
4. Cover with foil, then bake for 60 minutes until the chicken is done.
5. Serve with sour cream and chopped avocado.

Nutrition info:

550 calories, 31.5g fat, 54g protein, 12g carbs, 4g fiber, 8g net carbs

Dinner recipes

Turkey Meatball

Prep Time: 5 min

Cook Time: 15 min

Servings: 5 servings

Ingredients:

- 1-pound ground turkey
- One egg, whipped
- 2–4 tbsp flour
- Two cloves garlic, crushed
- 2 tbsp fresh herbs
- 3/4 tsp salt
- several grinds of fresh Black Pepper
- 2 tbsp butter, ghee, or coconut oil

Instructions:

1. In a large bowl, combine turkey meat, egg, flour, garlic, salt, and herbs and mix until well incorporated. Roll into small balls (about 1 1/2 inches). You'll get about 24-26 meatballs—heat 2 tbsp fat of choice in a large skillet on medium-high heat.
2. Cook meatballs for 3-4 minutes, until all sides are brown. You may need to do this in batches. Set aside.

Nutritional Info:

Fat: 14g, Carbohydrates: 344g, Protein: 24g, Calories: 357

Dinner recipes

Sausage stuffed bell peppers

Prep time: 15 minutes
Cook time: 45 minutes
Servings: 4

Ingredients:

- One medium head cauliflower, chopped
- One tablespoon olive oil
- 12 ounces ground Italian sausage
- One small yellow onion, chopped
- One teaspoon dried oregano
- Salt and pepper
- Four medium bell peppers

Instructions:

1. Preheat the oven to 350°f.
2. Pulse the cauliflower in a food processor into rice-like grains.
3. Heat the oil in a skillet over medium heat then add the cauliflower – cook for 6 to 8 minutes until tender.
4. Spoon the cauliflower rice into a bowl, then reheat the skillet.
5. Add the sausage and cook until browned, then drain the fat.
6. Stir the sausage into the cauliflower, then add the onion, oregano, salt, and pepper.
7. Slice the tops off the peppers, remove the seeds and pith, then spoon the sausage mixture into them.
8. Place the peppers upright in a baking dish, then cover the dish with foil.
9. Bake for 30 minutes, then uncover and bake 15 minutes more. Serve hot.

Nutrition info:

355 calories, 23.5g fat, 19g protein, 16.5g carbs, 6g fiber, 10.5g net carbs

Dinner recipes

Keto Chili Kicker

Prep Time: 5 min
Cook Time: 15 min
Servings: 2

Ingredients:
- 16 oz minced beef.
- Two avocados (chopped).
- One tomato finely chopped.
- One garlic clove crushed.
- 3 tbsp lime juice fresh.
- 2 tbsp red onion finely chopped.
- 1 tbsp coriander ground.
- 1 tbsp cumin ground.
- ½ tsp cayenne pepper.
- ½ tsp garlic powder.
- ¼ tsp black pepper.

Instructions:
1. In a large frying pan, add minced beef, coriander, cumin, cayenne pepper, and garlic powder. Fry for 6-8 minutes or until meat is thoroughly cooked.
2. In a bowl, mix avocados, tomatoes, crushed garlic, onion, lime juice, and black pepper; mix until well combined.
3. Put chili into a bowl and serve avocado salsa on top.

Nutrition info:
Fat: 15g, Carbohydrates: 4g, Protein: 35g, Calories: 330

Dinner recipes

Cauliflower crust meat lover's pizza

Prep time: 20 minutes
Cook time: 20 minutes
Servings: 2

Ingredients:

- One tablespoon butter
- 2 cups riced cauliflower
- Salt and pepper
- 1 ½ cups shredded mozzarella cheese, divided into 1 cup and ½ cup
- 1 cup fresh grated parmesan
- One teaspoon garlic powder
- One large egg white
- One teaspoon dried Italian seasoning
- ¼ cup low-carb tomato sauce
- 2 ounces sliced pepperoni
- 1-ounce diced ham
- Two slices bacon, cooked and crumbled

Instructions:

1. Preheat the oven to 400°f and line a baking sheet with parchment.
2. Heat the butter in a skillet over medium-high heat and add the cauliflower.
3. Season with salt and pepper, then cover and cook for 15 minutes, occasionally stirring, until very tender.
4. Spoon the cauliflower into a bowl and stir in ½ cup mozzarella along with the parmesan and garlic powder.
5. Stir in the egg white and Italian seasoning, then pour onto the baking sheet.
6. Shape the dough into a circle about ½-inch thick, then bake for 15 minutes.
7. Top with tomato sauce, along with the remaining mozzarella and the pepperoni, bacon, and ham.
8. Broil until the cheese is browned, then slice to serve.

Nutrition info:
560 calories, 40.5g fat, 41g protein, 11g carbs, 3g fiber, 8g net carbs

Dinner recipes

Spicy Salmon with Salsa

Prep Time: 5 min
Cook Time: 10 min
Servings: 2 servings

Ingredients:

- 4 salmon fillets.
- 1 tbsp olive oil.
- 4 tsp cajun seasoning.
- Two avocados chopped into small chunks.
- One jalapeno finely chopped.
- One red onion finely chopped.
- 1 tbsp lime juice fresh.
- 1 tbsp fresh coriander finely chopped.

Instructions:

1. Season both sides of salmon with Cajun seasoning.
2. Heat the oil in a large frying pan and fry the salmon until intensely golden brown; turn and repeat for the other side.
3. Mix the avocados, jalapenos, onion, coriander, and lime until well combined.
4. Serve with salmon.

Nutrition info:

Fat: 32g, Carbohydrates: 10g, Protein: 35g, Calories: 444

Dinner recipes

Pepper grilled ribeye with asparagus

Prep time: 5 minutes
Cook time: 15 minutes
Servings: 4

Ingredients:

- 1-pound asparagus, trimmed
- Two tablespoons olive oil
- Salt and pepper
- 1-pound ribeye steak
- One tablespoon coconut oil

Instructions:

1. Preheat the oven to 400°f and line a small baking sheet with foil.
2. Toss the asparagus with olive oil and spread it on the baking sheet.

3. Season with salt and pepper then place in the oven.
4. Rub the steak with the pepper and season with salt.
5. Melt the coconut oil in a cast-iron skillet and heat over high heat.
6. Add the steak and cook for 2 minutes, then turn it.
7. Transfer skillet to the oven and cook for 5 minutes or until the steak is done to the desired level.
8. Slice the steak and serve with the roasted asparagus.

Nutrition info:
380 calories, 25g fat, 35g protein, 4.5g carbs, 2.5g fiber, 2g net carbs

Dinner recipes

Cheesy Chicken Chunks

Prep Time: 5 min
Cook Time: 10 min
Servings: 3

Ingredients:
- 2 large chicken breasts (cut into strips).
- One large egg.
- ¾ cup parmesan cheese grated.
- ¾ cup almond flour.

Instructions:
- Preheat oven at 400 degrees.
- Mix the parmesan and flour.
- In a separate bowl, whisk the egg.
- Dip each strip of chicken into the egg mixture and then into the flour mixture. Place on a wire rack.
- Spray chicken with cooking spray and bake for 18-20 minutes or until browned and thoroughly cooked.

Nutrition info:
Fat: 24g, Carbohydrates: 2g, Protein: 41g, Calories: 398

Dinner recipes

Steak Kebabs with peppers and onions

Prep time: 30 minutes
Cook time: 10 minutes
Servings: 4

Ingredients:

- 1-pound beef sirloin, cut into 1-inch cubes
- ¼ cup olive oil
- Two tablespoons balsamic vinegar
- Salt and pepper
- One medium yellow onion, cut into chunks
- One medium red pepper, cut into chunks
- One medium green pepper, cut into chunks

Instructions:

1. Toss the steak cubes with the olive oil, balsamic vinegar, salt, and pepper.
2. Slide the cubes onto skewers with the peppers and onions.
3. Preheat a grill to high heat and oil the grates.
4. Grill the kebabs for 2 to 3 minutes on each side until done to your liking.

Nutrition info:
350 calories, 20g fat, 35g protein, 6.5g carbs, 1.5g fiber, 5g net carbs

Dinner recipes

Zingy Garlic Chicken Kebab

Prep Time: 5 min
Cook Time: 20 min
Servings: 6

Ingredients:

- 32 oz chicken breast (cut into 1-inch cubes).
- Four garlic cloves crushed.
- One lemon zested and juiced.
- ½ cup of almond milk.
- ¼ cup olive oil.
- ¼ cup fresh parsley finely chopped.
- ½ tsp salt.
- ¼ tsp black pepper.
- 1 tbsp mixed herbs dried.

Instructions:

1. In a large bowl, mix garlic, lemon, almond milk, olive oil, parsley, salt, Pepper, and herbs.
2. Add chicken cubes to the bowl and stir well to ensure all chicken is coated.
3. Chill in the fridge for 2-3 hours, occasionally stirring to ensure even coverage.
4. Fry the chicken in a large frying pan until browned and cooked.
5. Using wooden skewers, fill the skewer with chicken pieces.

Nutrition info:
Fat: 14g, Carbohydrates: 2g, Protein: 33g, Calories: 276

Dinner recipes

Lemon chicken kebabs with veggies

Prep time: 10 minutes
Cook time: 15 minutes
Servings: 4

Ingredients:

- 1-pound boneless chicken thighs, cut into cubes
- ¼ cup olive oil
- Two tablespoons lemon juice
- One teaspoon minced garlic
- Salt and pepper
- One large yellow onion, cut into 2-inch chunks
- One large red pepper, cut into 2-inch chunks
- One large green pepper, cut into 2-inch chunks

Instructions:

1. Toss the chicken with the olive oil, lemon juice, garlic, salt, and pepper.
2. Slide the chicken onto skewers with the onion and peppers.
3. Preheat a grill to medium-high heat and oil the grates.
4. Grill tea square for 2 to 3 minutes and yes side until the tea is chicken for 2 minutes.

Nutrition info:
360 calories, 21g fat, 34g protein, 8g carbs, 2g fiber, 6g net carbs

Dinner recipes

Antipasto Meat Sticks

Prep Time: 5 min
Cook Time: 10 min
Servings: 3

Ingredients:

- 4 slices salami.
- Four slices sandwich ham.
- Four slices pepperoni.
- 4 slices cheddar cheese.
- Four slices mozzarella.
- One handful lettuce (chopped)
- 2 tbsp olive oil.
- 1 tbsp apple cider vinegar.
- 1 tbsp mayonnaise.
- ½ tsp mixed herbs dried.

Instructions:

1. In 4 separate piles, layer the meat slices from biggest to smallest.
2. Spread with mayonnaise and add the cheese slices.
3. Sprinkle on lettuce.
4. Roll each pile into a tight sausage shape; secure with a toothpick.
5. In a dish, add olive oil, vinegar, and herbs to use as a dip for antipasto sticks.

Nutrition info:

Fat: 21g, Carbohydrates: 1g, Protein: 10g, Calories: 234

Dinner recipes

Cheesy-Meat Tapas

Prep Time: 5 min
Cook Time: 10 min
Servings: 2 servings

Ingredients:

- 8 oz prosciutto sliced.
- 8 oz chorizo sliced.
- 4 oz cheddar cheese cubed.
- 4 oz mozzarella cubed.
- 4 oz cucumber cubed.
- 2 oz red pepper sliced.

Instructions:

1. Arrange all items on a plate.
2. Enjoy.

Nutrition info:

Fat: 74g, Carbohydrates: 8g, Protein: 57g, Calories: 944

Dinner recipes

Tasty Salted Turnip Fries

Prep Time: 5 min
Cook Time: 10 min
Servings: 2

Ingredients:

- 16 oz turnips.
- 6 tbsp olive oil.
- 2 tsp onion powder.
- ½ tsp paprika.
- 1 tsp salt.

Instructions:

1. Preheat oven at 400 degrees.
2. Wash and peel the turnips; cut into ½ inch strips.
3. In a large bowl, toss the turnips in 2 tbsp of olive oil, salt, onion powder, and paprika.
4. Add remaining oil to a baking tray and heat in the oven for 5 minutes.
5. Bake for 25-30 minutes or until fries is golden brown and crispy.

Nutrition info:

Fat: 22g, Carbohydrates: 7g, Protein: 2g, Calories: 219

Dinner recipes

Overnight Oats

Prep Time: 5 min
Cook Time: 5 min
Servings: 3

Ingredients:

- 1 cup organic rolled oats
- 2 ½ cups Strawberry Cashew Milk
- 1 Tablespoon Chia seeds
- 1 Tablespoon Whole flax seeds

Instructions:

1. Place rolled oats, chia seeds, and flax seeds in a large bowl. Poor in 2 ½ cups of strawberry cashew milk (or preferred dairy, nut or seed milk) and stir well to combine. Cover and store in the fridge for 1 hour or overnight.
2. Check consistency and add additional Strawberry Cashew Milk as desired. Portion into individual containers. Add fresh strawberries, cashews, chia seeds, flax seeds, or extra Strawberry Cashew Milk as toppings. Enjoy immediately or store in airtight containers for up to 5 days.

Nutrition info:
Fat: 70g, Carbohydrates: 35g, Protein: 15g, Calories: 533

Keto Bonus Recipe

Strawberry Cashew Milk

Prep Time: 10 min
Cook Time: 5 min
Servings: 4 servings

Ingredients:

- 2 cups raw, unsalted cashews
- 1 pint of strawberries (2-2 ½ cups)
- 4 cups of filtered water
- Pinch of sea salt
- 1 T raw honey (optional)

Instructions:

1. Using a high-speed blender, add cashews and water to the pitcher.
2. While cashews are soaking, wash strawberries, trim to tops, and slice in half.
3. Add strawberries, sea salt, and optional sweetener. Blend on high for 1 minute till full incorporated and smooth.
4. Store in an airtight container in the fridge for up to 7 days.

Nutrition info:
Fat: 44g, Carbohydrates: 5g, Protein: 27g, Calories: 516

Keto Bonus Recipe

Coco-macadamia

Prep time: 5 minutes
Cook time: none
Servings: 16

Ingredients:
- 1 cup of coconut oil
- 1 cup smooth almond butter
- ½ cup unsweetened cocoa powder
- ¼ cup coconut flour
- Liquid stevia extract, to taste
- 16 whole macadamia nuts, raw

Instructions:

1. Melt the coconut oil and cashew butter together in a small saucepan.
2. Whisk in the cocoa powder, coconut flour, and liquid stevia to taste.
3. Remove from heat and let cool until it hardens slightly.
4. Divide the mixture into 16 even pieces.
5. Roll each piece into a ball around a macadamia nut and chill until ready to eat.

Nutrition info:
255 calories, 25.5g fat, 3.5g protein, 7g carbs, 3g fiber, 4g net carbs

Keto Bonus Recipe

Egg & Mackerel Breakfast Kick-Start

Prep Time: 5 min
Cook Time: 15 min
Servings: 2

Ingredients:

- 4 large eggs.
- Eight mackerel in tomato sauce.
- ½ red onion finely sliced.
- ¼ cup olive oil.
- 2 oz lettuce.
- 2 tbsp butter.
- Salt and pepper.

Instructions:

1. Melt butter in a frying pan and cook the eggs to your preference.
2. On a serving plate, place lettuce and top with onion. Add the eggs and mackerel to the plate.
3. Drizzle olive oil over the lettuce and season with salt and pepper.

Nutrition info:

Fat: 59g, Carbohydrates: 4.2g, Protein: 35g, Calories: 689,

Keto Bonus Recipe

Curry-roasted macadamia nuts

Prep time: 5 minutes
Cook time: 25 minutes
Servings: 8

Ingredients:

- 1 ½ tablespoon olive oil
- One tablespoon curry powder
- ½ teaspoon salt
- 2 cups macadamia nuts, raw

Instructions:

1. Preheat the oven to 300°f and line a baking sheet with parchment.
2. Whisk together the olive oil, curry powder, and salt in a mixing bowl.
3. Toss in the macadamia nuts to coat, then spread on the baking sheet.
4. Bake for 25 minutes until toasted, then cool to room temperature.

Nutrition info:

265 calories, 28g fat, 3g protein, 5g carbs, 3g fiber, 2g net carbs

Keto Bonus Recipe

The Magnificent Breakfast Mushroom

Prep Time: 5 min
Cook Time: 10 min
Servings: 2

Ingredients:

- 2 large deep cup mushrooms (stem removed).
- Four slices of bacon cooked and chopped.
- Two large eggs.
- 1/10 cup parmesan is grated.
- Cooking spray.

Instructions:

1. Preheat oven at 375 degrees.
2. On a baking tray, spray the mushrooms with cooking spray and bake for 10 minutes.
3. Split the bacon and parmesan between the two mushrooms and bake for an additional 5 minutes.
4. Crack an egg into each mushroom and bake for an additional 10 minutes.

Nutrition info:

Fat: 47g, Carbohydrates: 8g, Protein: 30g, Calories: 578

Keto Bonus Recipe

Coconut chia pudding

Prep time: 5 minutes
Cook time: none
Servings: 6

Ingredients:

- Two ¼ cups canned coconut milk
- One teaspoon vanilla extract
- Pinch salt
- ½ cup chia seeds

Instructions:

1. Combine the coconut milk, vanilla, and salt in a bowl.
2. Stir well and sweeten with stevia to taste.
3. Whisk in the chia seeds and chill overnight.
4. Spoon into bowls and serve with chopped nuts or fruit.

300 calories, 27.5g fat, 6g protein, 14.5g carbs, 10g fiber, 4.5g net carbs

Keto Bonus Recipe

Keto Crunchy Cauliflower Hash Browns

Prep Time: 5 min
Cook Time: 15 min
Servings: 4

Ingredients:

- 16 oz cauliflower (head grated).
- Three large eggs.
- ½ onion finely diced.
- 4 oz butter.
- 1 tsp salt.
- ¼ tsp black pepper.

Instructions:

1. Add all ingredients (except butter) to a large bowl and mix until well combined. Allow standing for 10 minutes.
2. Melt ¼ butter in a large frying pan. Add two scoops of cauliflower mixture; Carefully flatten until they are 3-4 inches in diameter.
3. Fry for 4-5 minutes on each side.
4. Repeat until all the mixture has gone.

Nutrition info:
Fat: 26g, Carbohydrates: 5g, Protein: 7g, Calories: 282,

Keto Bonus Recipe

Layered almond chocolate

Prep time: 10 minutes
Cook time: none
Servings: 12

Ingredients:

- ½ cup almond butter
- Six tablespoons coconut oil, divided
- One teaspoon vanilla extract
- Liquid stevia extract, to taste
- 4 ounces 90% dark chocolate, chopped
- 1-ounce toasted almonds, finely chopped

Instructions:

1. Melt the almond butter and two tablespoons of coconut oil together in a bowl.
2. Stir in the vanilla extract and sweeten with stevia to taste.
3. Divide the mixture into 12 silicone baking molds and chill until set.
4. Melt the remaining coconut oil with the dark chocolate and stir until
5. Smooth.
6. Spoon into the silicone molds over the almond butter layer.
7. Sprinkle with chopped almonds and chill until solid.
8. Pop the fat bombs out of the molds and store in an airtight container in the fridge.

Nutrition info:
160 calories, 16.5g fat, 2.5g protein, 4g carbs, 1.5g fiber, 2.5g net carbs

Keto Bonus Recipe

Baked Egg Breakfast Banquet

Prep Time: 5 min
Cook Time: 15 min
Servings: 2 servings

Ingredients:
- 2 large eggs.
- 3 oz minced beef.
- 2 oz cheddar cheese grated.

Instructions:
1. Preheat oven at 400 degrees.
2. Put the minced beef into a baking dish; make two holes in the mince and crack in the eggs.
3. Sprinkle the cheese over the top.
4. Bake for 10-15 minutes or until the eggs are cooked.

Nutrition info:
Fat: 36g, Carbohydrates: 2g, Protein: 40g, Calories: 498

Keto Bonus Recipe

Layered coco-chia

Prep time: 10 minutes
Cook time: none
Servings: 12

Ingredients:

½ cup coconut butter

Six tablespoons coconut oil, divided
Two tablespoons chia seeds
½ teaspoon coconut extract
Liquid stevia extract, to taste
4 ounces 90% dark chocolate, chopped

Instructions:

Melt the coconut butter and two tablespoons of coconut oil together in a bowl.
Stir in the chia seeds and coconut extract, then sweeten with stevia to taste.
Divide the mixture into 12 silicone baking molds and chill until set.
Melt the remaining coconut oil with the dark chocolate and stir until smooth.
Spoon into the silicone molds over the solid layer and chill until solid.
Pop the fat bombs out of the molds and store in an airtight container in the fridge.

Nutrition info:
215 calories, 21.5g fat, 2g protein, 6.5g carbs, 4.5g fiber, 2g net carbs

Keto Bonus Recipe

Paleo Lamb Meatballs

Prep Time: 5 min
Cook Time: 15 min
Servings: 2

Ingredients:

- 1-lb ground lamb
- One egg
- 2 tsp Organic Italian spice blend
- 1 tsp cumin powder
- 1 tsp coriander powder
- 3 tsp dried oregano
- 3 tsp whole fennel seeds
- 1 Tbsp fresh parsley, generous amount, minced
- ¼ tsp sea salt
- ¼ tsp coarse black pepper

Instructions:

1. Preheat oven to 400 degrees. Prepare a baking pan with parchment paper.
2. In a medium bowl, combine lamb, egg, and spices blend well with your hands—separate and roll into four even balls. Say a positive affirmation or word while forming the meatballs.

3. Place on the baking sheet and bake for 20 minutes. Enjoy immediately or store in an airtight container for up to 5 days.

Nutrition info:
Fat: 24g, Carbohydrates: 77g, Protein: 135g, Calories: 485,

Keto Bonus Recipe

Lemon meringue cookies

Prep time: 10 minutes
Cook time: 60 minutes
Servings: 8

Ingredients:

- Four large egg whites
- Pinch salt
- Liquid stevia extract, to taste
- One teaspoon lemon extract

Instructions:

1. Preheat the oven to 225°f and line a baking sheet with parchment.
2. Beat the egg whites in a bowl until soft peaks form.
3. Add the salt and stevia, then beat until stiff peaks form.
4. Fold in the lemon extract, then spoon into a piping bag.
5. Pipe the mixture onto the baking sheet in small rounds.
6. Bake for 50 to 60 minutes until dry, then open the oven door and cool 20 minutes.

Nutrition info:
Ten calories, 0g fat, 2g protein, 0g carbs, 0g fiber, 0g net carbs

Keto Bonus Recipe

Jolly Good Egg & Bacon Sandwich

Prep Time: 5 min
Cook Time: 10 min
Servings: 1
Ingredients:
- Cooking spray.
- Two large eggs.

- 1 tbsp coconut flour.
- 1 tbsp butter salted.
- ¼ tsp baking powder.
- One slice cheddar cheese.
- Two slices of bacon (grilled)

Instructions:

1. Place butter in the microwave for 30 seconds or until melted.
2. Let the butter cool slightly. Mix in 1 egg, coconut flour, and baking powder; microwave for one and a half minutes.
3. Allow bread to cool and slice to make two equally thin slices.
4. Using the cooking spray, fry the remaining egg to your preference. Grill the bread until toasted and crunchy.
5. Assemble the sandwich placing a slice of toast on the bottom, cheese, bacon, and fried egg; top with remaining toast.

Nutrition info:
Fat: 39g, Carbohydrates: 6g, Protein: 28g, Calories: 490,

Keto Bonus Recipe

Coconut macaroons

Prep time: 10 minutes
Cook time: 10 minutes
Servings: 10

Ingredients:

- ½ cup unsweetened shredded coconut
- ¼ cup almond flour
- Two tablespoons powdered erythritol
- One tablespoon coconut oil
- One teaspoon vanilla extract
- ½ teaspoon coconut extract
- Three large egg whites

Instructions:

1. Preheat the oven to 400°f and line a baking sheet with parchment.
2. Combine the almond flour, coconut, and erythritol in a bowl.
3. In a separate bowl, melt the coconut oil, then whisk in the extracts.
4. Stir the two mixtures together until well combined.
5. Beat the egg whites in a bowl until stiff peaks form, then fold into the batter.
6. Spoon onto the baking sheet in even-sized mounds.
7. Bake for 7 to 9 minutes until the cookies browned on the edges.

Nutrition info:
105 calories, 9g fat, 2.5g protein, 3g carbs, 2g fiber, 1g net carbs

Keto Bonus Recipe

Keto-Buzz Blueberry Pancakes

Prep Time: 5 min
Cook Time: 20 min
Servings: 3

Ingredients:
- Three large eggs.
- ½ cup almond flour.
- ¼ cup of milk.
- ¼ cup of fresh blueberries.
- 2 tbsp coconut flour.
- 2 tbsp sweetener granulated.
- 1 tsp cinnamon ground.
- ½ tsp baking powder.

Instructions:
1. Add all ingredients (except blueberries) to a blender and mix until a thick batter is formed.
2. Add the blended mixture to a bowl and stir in blueberries.
3. Grease a large non-stick frying pan and allow the pot to get hot over medium heat.
4. Pour ¼ cup of the mixture into the hot pan, allow to cook for 2 - 3 minutes, or until the edges start to crisp and turn lightly browned. Flip and repeat.
5. Repeat the process using the remaining batter.

Nutrition info:
Fat: 7g, Carbohydrates: 4g, Protein: 7g, Calories: 132,

Keto Bonus Recipe

Crunchy ginger cookies

Prep time: 10 minutes
Cook time: 15 minutes
Servings: 16

Ingredients:

- 1 cup coconut butter
- One large egg
- One teaspoon vanilla extract

- ½ cup powdered erythritol
- ½ teaspoon ground ginger
- ½ teaspoon baking soda
- ¼ teaspoon ground nutmeg
- Pinch salt

Instructions:

1. Preheat the oven to 350°f and line a baking sheet with parchment.
2. Place the coconut butter in a food processor with the egg and vanilla.
3. Blend smooth, then add the erythritol, ginger, baking soda, nutmeg, and salt.
4. Pulse until it forms a dough, then shape into 16 small balls.
5. Place the balls on the baking sheet and flatten slightly.
6. Bake for 12 to 15 minutes until the edges browned then cold.

Nutrition info:
190 calories, 18g fat, 2.5g protein, 7g carbs, 5g fiber, 2g net Carbs

Keto Bonus Recipe

What Waffle!

Prep Time: 5 min
Cook Time: 15min
Servings: 6

Ingredients:

- 2 large eggs.
- 2 cups almond flour.
- 1 ½ cups almond milk warm.
- ⅓ cup of butter melted.
- 2 tbsp erythritol.
- 4 tsp baking powder.
- 1 tsp vanilla extract.
- 1 tsp salt.

Instructions:

1. Mix baking powder, salt, and almond flour until well combined.
2. In a separate bowl, whisk the eggs until well combined.
3. Take the lukewarm almond milk and mix with the eggs, adding melted butter, erythritol, and vanilla extract.
4. Stir the egg mixture into the flour mixture until a dough is formed. Let sit for several minutes.
5. Cook in a hot waffle iron for 6-8 minutes.

Nutrition info:
Fat: 31g, Carbohydrates: 8g, Protein: 11g, Calories: 345,

Keto Bonus Recipe

Peppermint dark chocolate fudge

Prep time: 15 minutes
Cook time: none
Servings: 16

Ingredients:

- ½ cup coconut butter
- ⅓ cup coconut oil
- 4 ounces dark chocolate chips
- One teaspoon peppermint extract
- Liquid stevia extract, to taste

Instructions:

1. Combine the coconut butter, coconut oil, and dark chocolate in a double boiler over low heat.
2. Cook until the ingredients are melted, then stir until smooth.
3. Whisk in the peppermint extract and sweeten with stevia to taste.
4. Spread the mixture in a parchment-lined baking dish and chill until firm.
5. Remove the fudge from the dish and cut into squares to serve.

Nutrition info:

165 calories, 15.5g fat, 1.5g protein, 8.5g carbs, 2.5g fiber, 6g net carbs

Keto Bonus Recipe

Bacon & Egg Pick-me-up

Prep Time: 5 min
Cook Time: 10 min
Servings: 4

Ingredients:
- 8 large eggs.
- 5 oz bacon slices.
- A handful of cherry tomatoes halved.

Instructions:
1. In a large frying pan, fry bacon rashers until crispy. Set aside, leaving bacon fat in the pan.
2. Crack the eggs into the frying pan and fry eggs to your preferred taste.
3. When eggs are nearly cooked, throw in the cherry tomatoes and fry until lightly browned.

Nutrition info:

Fat: 24g, Carbohydrates: 1g, Protein: 17g, Calories: 274,

Keto Bonus Recipe

Creamy queso dip

Prep time: 15 minutes
Cook time: 5 minutes
Servings: 8

Ingredients:

- 4 ounces chorizo, crumbled
- One clove garlic, minced
- ¼ cup heavy cream
- 6 ounces shredded white cheddar cheese
- 2 ounces shredded pepper jack cheese
- ¼ teaspoon xanthan gum
- Pinch salt
- One jalapeno, seeded and minced
- One small tomato, diced

Instructions:

1. Cook the chorizo in a skillet until evenly browned, then spoon into a bowl.
2. Reheat the skillet on medium-low heat and add the garlic – cook for 30 seconds.
3. Stir in the heavy cream, then add the cheese a little at a time, often stirring until it melts together.
4. Sprinkle with xanthan gum and salt, then stir well and cook until thickened.
5. Stir in the tomato and jalapeno, then serve with veggies for dipping.

Nutrition info:
195 calories, 16g fat, 11g protein, 1.5g carbs, 0.5g fiber, 1g net carbs

Keto Bonus Recipe

No-Fuss Egg Medley Muffins

Prep Time: 5 min
Cook Time: 20 min
Servings: 5

Ingredients:

- 12 large eggs.
- One onion finely chopped.
- 6 oz cheddar cheese grated.
- 5 oz bacon cooked and diced.
- Pinch salt and pepper.

Instructions:

1. Preheat the oven at 175 degrees and grease a 12-hole muffin tray.

2. Equally, place onion and bacon to the bottom of each muffin tray hole.
3. In a large bowl, whisk the eggs, cheese, salt, and pepper.
4. Pour the egg mixture into each hole; on top of the onions and bacon.
5. Bake for 15-20 minutes, until browned and firm to the touch.

Nutrition info:
Fat: 28g, Carbohydrates: 2g, Protein: 22g, Calories: 333,

Keto Bonus Recipe

Matcha coconut

Prep time: 10 minutes
Cook time: none
Servings: 16

Ingredients:

- ½ cup of coconut oil
- ½ cup coconut butter
- ¼ cup canned coconut milk
- ½ teaspoon vanilla extract
- Pinch salt
- ½ cup shredded unsweetened coconut
- Two teaspoons matcha powder

Instructions:

1. Combine the coconut oil, coconut butter, coconut milk, and a pinch of matcha powder in a large mixing bowl.
2. Add the vanilla and salt, then beat on high speed until fluffy.
3. Transfer to the refrigerator and chill for an hour.
4. Scoop the mixture into 16 small portions and roll them into balls.
5. Combine the coconut and matcha in a bowl and roll the balls in it.
6. Chill until firm, then store in an airtight container.

Nutrition info:
170 calories, 17.5g fat, 1.5g protein, 4g carbs, 3g fiber, 1g net carbs

Keto Bonus Recipe

Charming Cream Cheese

Prep Time: 5 min
Cook Time: 5 min
Servings: 1 servings

Ingredients:

- 2 large eggs
- 2 oz cream cheese.
- 1 tsp granulated sugar substitute.
- ½ tsp ground cinnamon.

Instructions:

1. Blend all ingredients until smooth. Allow resting for 2 minutes.
2. Grease a large frying pan and pour in ¼ of the mixture.
3. Cook for 2 minutes until golden, flip and cook for an additional minute.
4. Repeat the process until all mixture has gone.

Nutrition info:

Fat: 30g, Carbohydrates: 3g, Protein: 16g, Calories: 346,

Keto Bonus Recipe

Chocolate-dipped pecan

Prep time: 10 minutes
Cook time: none
Servings: 16

Ingredients:

- 1 cup coconut butter
- 1 cup of canned coconut milk
- 1 cup finely chopped pecans
- One teaspoon vanilla extract
- Liquid stevia extract, to taste
- ¼ cup chopped dark chocolate
- ½ teaspoon palm shortening

Instructions:

1. Combine the coconut butter and coconut milk in a small saucepan over low heat.
2. When melted, stir in the pecans and vanilla, then sweeten to taste.
3. Remove from heat and chill for 1 to 2 hours until firm.
4. Divide the mixture into 16 portions and roll them into small balls.
5. Melt the dark chocolate in the microwave with the palm shortening.
6. Dip the balls in the chocolate and place them on a plate.

7. Chill until the chocolate hardened, then serve.

Nutrition info:
245 calories, 24.5g fat, 3g protein, 9.5g carbs, 5.5g fiber, 4g net carbs

Keto Bonus Recipe

Stay Right There - Soldiers & Egg
Prep Time: 5 min
Cook Time: 15 min
Servings: 1

Ingredients:
- 1 large egg.
- 2 oz cheddar cheese cut in chunky wedges.

Instructions:
1. Gently place the egg in a lidded saucepan of cold water, bring to the boil.
2. When the water is boiling excessively, turn off the heat and remove the pan away from the heat.
3. To create a soft and runny center, leave the egg sitting in hot water for 4 minutes.
4. Take the egg out of the water and crack off the top of the egg. Use the cheese sticks to dunk into the egg.

Nutrition info:
Fat: 22g, Carbohydrates: 1g, Protein: 17g, Calories: 270,

Keto Bonus Recipe

Chocolate-dipped coconut

Prep time: 10 minutes
Cook time: none
Servings: 5

Ingredients:

- 1 cup coconut butter
- 1 cup of canned coconut milk
- ¾ cup unsweetened shredded coconut
- Two teaspoons vanilla extract
- Liquid stevia extract, to taste
- ¼ cup chopped dark chocolate
- ½ teaspoon palm shortening

Instructions:

1. Combine the coconut butter and coconut milk in a small saucepan over low heat.
2. When melted, stir in the coconut and vanilla, then sweeten to taste.
3. Remove from heat and chill for 1 to 2 hours until firm.
4. Divide the mixture into 16 portions and roll them into small balls.
5. Melt the dark chocolate in the microwave with the palm shortening.
6. Dip the balls in the chocolate and place them on a plate.
7. Chill until the chocolate hardened, then serve.

Nutrition info:
300 calories, 28g fat, 3g protein, 11.5g carbs, 7g fiber, 4.5g net carbs

Keto Bonus Recipe

Chocolate sun butter

Prep time: 5 minutes
Cook time: none
Servings: 6

Ingredients:

- 1 cup of coconut oil
- 1 cup sunflower seed butter
- ½ cup unsweetened cocoa powder, divided
- ¼ cup coconut flour
- Liquid stevia extract, to taste

Instructions:

1. Melt the coconut oil and sunflower seed butter together in a small saucepan.
2. Whisk in ¼ cup of the cocoa powder along with the coconut flour and liquid stevia to taste.
3. Remove from heat and let cool until it hardens slightly.
4. Divide the mixture into 16 even pieces and roll into balls then place on a plate.
5. Roll the fat bombs in the remaining cocoa powder to coat and chill.

Nutrition info:
230 calories, 22g fat, 4g protein, 8g carbs, 2g fiber, 6g net carbs

Keto Bonus Recipe

Cinnamon mug cake

Prep time: 5 minutes
Cook time: 1 minute

Servings: 4

Ingredients:

- ⅓ cup almond flour
- One tablespoon powdered erythritol
- ½ teaspoon baking powder
- ¼ teaspoon ground cinnamon
- Pinch salt
- One large egg
- One tablespoon water
- One tablespoon coconut oil
- ½ teaspoon vanilla extract

Instructions:

1. Combine the almond flour, erythritol, baking powder, cinnamon, and salt.
2. In a separate bowl, whisk together the egg, water, coconut oil, and vanilla.
3. Stir the two mixtures together and pour into a greased coffee mug.
4. Cook in the microwave on high for 1 minute until done. Serve warm.

Nutrition info:
395 calories, 36g fat, 13.5g protein, 8.5g carbs, 4g fiber, 4.5g net carbs

Keto Bonus Recipe

Raspberry coconut mousse

Prep time: 15 minutes
Cook time: none
Servings: 6

Ingredients:
- 1 ½ cup cashews, raw
- Three tablespoons lemon juice
- Three tablespoons water
- 1 ½ tablespoons coconut oil, melted
- 1 cup of canned coconut milk (solids only)
- One teaspoon vanilla extract
- Liquid stevia extract, to taste
- ½ cup fresh raspberries, mashed slightly

Instructions:
1. Combine the cashews, lemon juice, water, and coconut oil in a blender and blend until smooth.

2. Beat the coconut milk with a hand mixer until stiff peaks form, then beat in the vanilla and stevia to taste.
3. Fold the whipped coconut milk into the cashew mixture, then fold in the berries.
4. Spoon into jars and chill for at least 1 hour before serving.

Nutrition info:
325 calories, 29g fat, 6.5g protein, 15g carbs, 2.5g fiber, 12.5g net carbs

Keto Bonus Recipe

Avocado Guacamole Breakfast Sandwich
Prep Time: 5 min
Cook Time: 20 min
Servings: 1

Ingredients:
- 6 slices bacon.
- Two avocados.
- Two small onions diced.
- 2 tbsp lime juice.
- 2 tbsp garlic powder.
- Cooking spray.

Instructions:
1. Preheat the oven at 180 degrees.
2. Spray a baking tray with cooking spray, cook the bacon 15-20 minutes until crispy.
3. Remove seeds from avocados; in a massive bowl, mash the avocado flesh with a fork.
4. Add onions, garlic, and lime juice; mash until well combined.
5. Allow the crispy bacon to cool and place one slice on a plate; top with 2 tbsp of avocado guacamole. Place another bacon slice on top and add another 2 tbsp of guacamole and top with bacon. Repeat to make another sandwich.

Nutrition info:
Fat: 46g, Carbohydrates: 11g, Protein: 23g, Calories: 544,

Keto Bonus Recipe

Cinnamon-spiced pumpkin bars

Prep time: 15 minutes
Cook time: 20
Servings: 6

Ingredients:

- ½ cup of coconut oil

- 4 ounces cream cheese, softened
- ¼ cup powdered erythritol
- 1 ½ teaspoon ground cinnamon
- ¼ cup pumpkin puree

Instructions:

1. Combine the coconut oil and cream cheese in a saucepan over medium-low heat.
2. Melt the ingredients, then stir well – transfer to a mixing bowl.
3. Beat in the erythritol and cinnamon, then spread in a dish lined with parchment.
4. Drizzle the pumpkin puree over the mixture and swirl with a knife.
5. Chill for 4 hours or until solid, then cut into bars to serve.

Nutrition info:
225 calories, 25g fat, 1.5g protein, 2g carbs, 0.5g fiber, 1.5g net carbs

Keto Bonus Recipe

Perfect Peanut Butter Breakfast Balls
Prep Time: 5 min
Cook Time: 15 min
Servings: 4

Ingredients:
- Two cups peanut butter smooth.
- ¾ cup coconut flour.
- ½ cup monk fruit sweetened maple syrup.

Instructions:
1. Line a large baking tray with greaseproof paper.
2. In a large bowl, mix all ingredients until a thick batter is formed.
3. Mold the batter into small balls and place them on the baking tray.
4. Refrigerate 40-60 minutes until firm.

Nutrition info:
Fat: 15g, Carbohydrates: 7g, Protein: 8g, Calories: 173,

Keto Bonus Recipe

Classic guacamole dip

Prep time: 15 minutes
Cook time: none
Servings: 4

Ingredients:

- Two medium avocados pitted
- One small yellow onion, diced
- One small tomato, diced
- ¼ cup fresh chopped cilantro
- One tablespoon fresh lime juice
- One jalapeno, seeded and minced
- One clove garlic, minced
- Salt
- Sliced veggies to serve

Instructions:

1. Spoon the avocado flesh into a bowl and mash slightly.
2. Stir in the onion, tomato, cilantro, lime juice, garlic, and jalapeno.
3. Season with salt to taste and spoon into a bowl – serve with sliced veggies.

Nutrition info:
220 calories, 20g fat, 2.5g protein, 12g carbs, 7.5g fiber, 4.5g net carbs

Keto Bonus Recipe

Tantalizing Tuna & Spinach Mix

Prep Time: 5 min
Cook Time: 15 min
Servings: 2

Ingredients:

- Four large eggs.
- Ten tins of olive oil.
- ½ cup mayonnaise.
- One avocado (sliced).
- One onion finely diced.
- Salt and pepper (to season).

Instructions:

1. Bring a large pan of water to the boil and lower in the eggs—Cook for 8 minutes.
2. In a bowl, mix tuna, mayonnaise, onion, salt, and pepper.
3. Chop the hard-boiled eggs into halves and place them on a plate with avocado slices and spinach.
4. Place the tuna mixture on top of spinach.

Nutrition info:

Fat: 79g, Carbohydrates: 3g, Protein: 53g, Calories: 952

With over 120 recipes contained herein, the whole idea here is to give you a boost in terms of the choice of food that you will get to enjoy beyond the 28-day meal plan provided. Designed to start a keto diet comfortably, you will find that the meal plan gradually becomes familiar to you. Follow the format of preparing keto-friendly, delicious foods that will serve you well in this ketogenic weight loss journey.

Once you have completed the meal plan, please feel free to mix and match the recipes here to create your very own meal plans! Always remember to keep the macronutrient numbers in mind and do not go overboard with the daily calorie intake. Overeating can still pack on the pounds, whether you are on keto or not.

Few Hacks You Might Benefit From

Stay hydrated – According to the United States National Library of Medicine, an adult person should drink between 2.7 to 3.7 liters of water per day. Be careful of liquid calories on a ketogenic diet. Avoid alcohol and sweetened drinks; you can satisfy your thirst with sparkling water (with added fresh lemon juice), full-fat yogurt, or ice tea. Eat fresh vegetables that are naturally high in water content. As many keto-ers, I experienced dry mouth and bad breath, too; they are common symptoms of ketosis. How I get rid of ketosis breath? The trick is to brush regularly, chew sugar-free gum, and drink more water.

Fat coffee – This is my little secret to burning fat faster. A cup of coffee with a tablespoon of butter gives me a prolonged energy hit until lunchtime. I love its creaminess and distinctly aftertaste, and I am impressed by its results. It may sound crazy, but try it once, and you will fall in love with "fat black."

Keep it simple – The key to a successful ketogenic diet is making simple tweaks to your lifestyle. Make a simple ketogenic meal plan to get yourself into a routine; stick to easy recipes such as salads and soups. Go for simple snacks, too. Declutter and simplify your kitchen, and choose quick meals to cook at home. Let go of control, relax, and go outside. Getting fresh air and spending time with family or pets will help make you more likely to stick to your diet.

CONCLUSION

One of the primary keys to any successful diet or lifestyle change has always been the recipes that fit in with the principles of the diet. I am sure there are many ways to achieve ketosis and to attain that weight loss goal. However, you do not want to get there by just having the same old dishes over and over again.

Variety is the name of the game here, which is crucial in ensuring the sustainability of the ketogenic diet. With the flavorful and delicious recipes found in this step by step keto cookbook, they will be useful additions for any keto dieter at any stage of their ketogenic journey. I have yet to see anyone complain about having too many easy yet delicious recipes!

For the beginners who have gotten this recipe cookbook, it would be quite useful for you to take the 28-day meal plan as a helpful guide. Still, you should step out from that comfort zone sooner or later as you progress along your keto adventure! Multiple recipes for it that you can pick and choose the most interesting ones on your palate.

A FINAL NOTE

We have arrived at this juncture, and I am so glad that you have chosen to take the steps needed on this ketogenic journey. This book and its contents, I hope, will be able to give you step by step actionable value, as always, for your progress toward nutritional ketosis.

More importantly, it is also my hope that the book has also given you the confidence booster and has built up your commitment to stay on a diet. Like I said in my other book, Ketogenic Diet. The Step by Step Guide for Beginners: Optimal Path to Effective Weight Loss, the benefits of ketosis await, and if health is wealth, you should be getting wealthy pretty soon! There will be other books coming out on the ketogenic diet from me, so do look out for them. In the meantime, if you have enjoyed this book

Thank you, stay healthy and happy!

Printed in Great Britain
by Amazon